The set of the Westside Theatre production of "The Food Chain." Set design by Tom Lynch.

THE
FOOD
CHAIN

BY NICKY SILVER

DRAMATISTS
PLAY SERVICE
INC.

THE FOOD CHAIN
was originally produced by
Robert V. Straus, Randall L. Wreghitt, Annette Niemtzow
Michael Jackowitz
in association with
Evangeline Morphos, Nancy Richards

THE FOOD CHAIN was produced by Robert V. Straus, Randall L. Wreghitt, Annette Niemtzow and Michael Jackowitz in association with Evangeline Morphos and Nancy Richards, with associate producers Kathlene O'Grady, Gilford Freely Productions, Andrew Barrett, Terri Adams, Fanny M. Mandelberger, Richard Kornberg and Pope Entertainment Group, Inc., at the Westside Theatre in New York City, on August 24, 1995. It was directed by Robert Falls; the scene design was by Tom Lynch; the costume design was by William Ivey Long; the lighting design was by Kenneth Posner; the sound design was by Duncan Edwards/Ben Rubin and the production stage manager was Allison Sommers. The cast was as follows:

AMANDA .... Hope Davis
BEA .... Phyllis Newman
FORD .... Rudolf Martin
SERGE .... Patrick Fabian
OTTO .... Tom McGowan

THE FOOD CHAIN received its premiere at the Woolly Mammoth Theater (Howard Shalwitz, Artistic Director) in Washington D.C., on July 15, 1994. It was directed by Nicky Silver; the set design was by James Kronzer; the costume design was by Howard Vincent Kurtz; the lighting design was by Martha Mountain and the production stage manager was Anne Theisen. The cast was as follows:

AMANDA .... Kate Flemming
BEA .... Cam Magee
FORD .... James Whalen
SERGE .... Christopher Lane
OTTO .... Rob Leo Roy

3

CHARACTERS

AMANDA DOLOR — Early thirties. A very attractive, high-strung intellectual. She is mercurial and has a terrific verbal capacity. It is important that she be very thin.

BEA — Mid-fifties. A Jewish matron with a heavy Long Island accent. She is abrasive and easily offended.

FORD DOLOR — Mid-thirties. A strikingly handsome man, Ford is a filmmaker and a man of ideas, not words.

SERGE STUBIN — Thirty. Serge is a sexual being, and as a runway model, he must be good-looking, although it is possible that he is less attractive than his confidence would indicate. Although intellectually out of his league with Amanda, Serge is far from stupid.

OTTO WOODNICK — Mid-thirties. Hugely overweight. Otto is flamboyant, Jewish, insecure in the extreme and full of rage. He is a verbal tornado, quite out of control.

SETTING

Scene 1: AMANDA
The Dolor living room in New York City, late at night.

Scene 2: OTTO
Serge's studio apartment, the same night.

Scene 3: FATTY AND SKINNY LAY IN BED
The Dolor living room, the next morning.

AUTHOR'S NOTE

Having worked on a couple of productions of THE FOOD CHAIN, and directed one myself, without negating the flexibility of any text there are several things I have learned about the play.

In Scene 1, Bea is on the phone and must appear as her phone is ringing. There are several solutions to this. In the original production, where budget was a grave concern, her cubicle appeared magically in the New York skyline. As her phone rang, Amanda's drapes parted revealing Bea, where previously there had only been buildings. When Amanda hung up on Bea, the drapes closed. In the New York production, a section of Amanda's apartment revolved revealing Bea and then revolved again when the call was over. I can imagine many solutions to this, but it is important that Bea be a presence on stage.

It is also important that Amanda have a speaker phone as she must be free to travel unhindered.

Also, Otto must be padded. I am not suggesting that only a thin actor can play the part. But he must be padded and padded to a degree that is slightly absurd. It is somewhat off-putting for an audience if they think the actor is actually as fat as the character needs to be. The audience will feel guilty for laughing at him and, thus, must be told, at the outset, that his mammoth size is a theatrical device.

As with many of my plays THE FOOD CHAIN juxtaposes several theatrical styles. What is important, I have found, is that the emotional reality never be forgotten. This is particularly true for THE FOOD CHAIN, as the third scene escalates so clearly into a realm of pure farce. As outrageous as Otto is (and the others for that matter) it is really Amanda's chore to ground the play in real need, right off the bat, and allow the growing urgency of that need to elevate the play to manic hights. She is the stylistic bridge.

In the interest of accuracy, I have included an alternate ending in this edition. This secondary ending was used in the play's premiere in Washington, D.C. It is my feeling that both endings work, despite one being much darker than the other, and I have decided to include them both.

Once again I find myself compelled to thank several people who helped bring this play to life. They include George Lane, Mary Meagher, Jill Westmorland, Michael Smith, James Bart Upchurch, III and Chuck Coggins. In Washington I was so fortunate to have a superb cast and I must acknowledge Nancy Turner Hensely and Rick Fiori, the producing associates, who cared about the play as if they'd written it. In New York it was my great good luck to have the cast listed above, all of whom made the production and the experience a dream. Not to mention the extravagantly gifted Robert Falls, who is just a riot.

THE FOOD CHAIN

SCENE 1

AMANDA

The lights come up on the Dolor living room. It is night. The room is decorated in an extremely young, "hip" manner. There is a hallway to the bedroom, a kitchen area, the main entrance and a powder room. Amanda is pacing, smoking a cigarette. She is listening to some sad, sophisticated jazz, wearing a tee-shirt and leggings or casual pants. After a moment, she goes to the phone and dials.

AMANDA. *(Into the phone.)* Hello, Bi — Damn. Hello, Binky. This is Amanda. If you're asleep, don't get up. If you're out, don't call me back. *(She looks at the phone as if she's just spoken gibberish and hangs up. She gets a New York Yellow Pages from a bookcase and looks up a number. She turns off the music and returns to the phone. She dials. This done, she presses a button which puts the call on speaker phone. We hear the ringing, and Bea is revealed.)*

BEA. Hello, Contact.

AMANDA. Yes, hello. *(Pause.)*

BEA. *(Irritated.)* This is Contact. Can I help you?

AMANDA. Yes. Well, probably not. I mean, I can't imagine how you could. I just, I wanted someone to talk to and it seemed to late to call anyone —

BEA. What's your address?

AMANDA. Pardon me?

BEA. What is your address?

AMANDA. Why do you ask?

BEA. This is a crisis hotline. I need your address.

AMANDA. I don't see how that's relevant.

BEA. I am not allowed to talk to you without an address.

AMANDA. I don't know that I want you —

BEA. *(A threat.)* I'm hanging up.

AMANDA. 241 West 21st Street.

BEA. That was so painful?

AMANDA. I just don't see the purpose —

BEA. Have you swallowed anything?

AMANDA. I just wanted to talk to someone.

BEA. What floor are you on?

AMANDA. Six.

BEA. Is the window looking more and more inviting?

AMANDA. I believe you have the wrong idea.

BEA. You have any firearms?

AMANDA. Firearms?

BEA. You know, guns, whatnot.

AMANDA. Certainly not.

BEA. *(Irritated.)* Are you lying to me? I will not tolerate being lied to!

AMANDA. I'm not going to do anything drastic.

BEA. Oh people say that. They always say that. People lie.

AMANDA. I assure you, I have no intention of —

BEA. Last week, Tuesday, I think, Tuesday or Wednesday, I can't remember — I'm on the phone forty-five minutes with this young man, *forty-five minutes,* and he's swearing up and down that he has no intention of doing anything — and after all that time, *mittin-drinnen,* out he sails. Right out the window. Dead.

AMANDA. Oh my.

BEA. *(A fact.)* People lie.

AMANDA. What was troubling him?

BEA. Oh, I can't remember. Something. Something was wrong with him. Who can keep it straight. But I tell you, I felt *VERY* betrayed!

AMANDA. I won't jump out the window.

BEA. That's why I'm on graveyard. I had a perfectly lovely shift: six to ten. After the talk shows and before the news. Now, I'm on graveyard.

AMANDA. I'm sorry.

BEA. I felt very betrayed.

AMANDA. I understand.

BEA.   Right out the window. Splattered. Dead. I heard the whole thing. It was terrible. What can I do for you, darling?

AMANDA. I just wanted to — talk to someone.

BEA.   You're lonely?

AMANDA. Well, I wouldn't say that.

BEA.   No. You're calling strangers in the middle of the night, but you're not lonely.

AMANDA. All right, I'm lonely.

BEA.   Well, let me tell you, *everyone's* lonely, my dear — what's your name?

AMANDA. Amanda.

BEA.   Amanda, loneliness is my oxygen. I breath loneliness. I'm Bea, and you don't know what loneliness is until you've walked a mile in my shoes. You haven't tasted loneliness, you haven't been in the same state with it. I lost my husband several years ago — I don't want to dwell. *Allif a sholem.* So what's the trouble?

AMANDA. My husband is ... gone.

BEA.   Gone? You mean dead gone? What do you mean? Be specific.

AMANDA. No, no. He's just gone.

BEA.   Is he missing? D'you call the police? Not that they'll do anything.

AMANDA. I haven't called the police. I mean, he's fine. He called me to say he was fine. He said he needed some time to work.

BEA.   When was that?

AMANDA. Two weeks ago.

BEA.   How long you been married?

AMANDA. Three weeks.

BEA.   And he's been missing?

AMANDA. Two weeks.

BEA.   I see.

AMANDA. He's working on a film. He writes films.

BEA.   Did he write *Howard's End?*

AMANDA. *(Bewildered.)* No.

BEA.   Too bad. I loved that picture. That is a beautiful picture. Did you see that picture?

AMANDA. No.

BEA. Ya should see it. See it on the big screen if you can. It was a lovely, lovely picture.

AMANDA. *(Testy.)* Well, I didn't see it.

BEA. Oh.

AMANDA. He makes small, independent films.

BEA. Did you see *Enchanted April?*

AMANDA. No.

BEA. Me neither. I'm dying to.

AMANDA. *(Lighting another cigarette.)* The point is —

BEA. Are you smoking?

AMANDA. Why?

BEA. Oh it's a terrible habit. You mustn't smoke. How old are ya darling?

AMANDA. Thirty.

BEA. You have your whole life ahead of ya, which, if you stop smoking could be a long, wonderful adventure.

AMANDA. I'm not smoking.

BEA. I heard you.

AMANDA. I have asthma. I wheeze sometimes.

BEA. Are you lying to me!?

AMANDA. No. I'm not. I'm not. I swear.

BEA. Did you see *Room With a View?*

AMANDA. Yes.

BEA. Oh was that a wonderful picture? Did you love that picture?

AMANDA. It was very good.

BEA. I loved that picture. So let me understand. You've been married three weeks and your husband's been missing for two of them?

AMANDA. Correct.

BEA. Did your husband — what's his name?

AMANDA. Ford.

BEA. That's a beautiful name! I love that name. Did Ford — I love saying it — did Ford tell you where he was going?

AMANDA. Well, it was a Monday. We'd spent the week on Martha's Vineyard. You see, it was our honeymoon and Ford has a friend who owns a house on Martha's Vineyard, which he never uses —

BEA. What's his name?

AMANDA. Who?

BEA. The friend, the friend with the house.

AMANDA. Why?

BEA. Maybe I know him.

AMANDA. Lillian.

BEA. *His* name is Lillian?

AMANDA. Yes.

BEA. Go figure.

AMANDA. In any event, we spent the week at Lillian's house. It was our honeymoon.

BEA. How was the sex?

AMANDA. It was good.

BEA. When you say "good," you mean what, exactly?

AMANDA. I mean it was good.

BEA. We'll come back to that. So you're in the city with Ford — I love that name!

AMANDA. Yes. We're back in the city. It's Monday morning. We had breakfast. And after breakfast, he told me that he wanted to go for a walk. So naturally, I started to put my shoes on. I thought he meant together — but he said, he wanted to go alone. He was working on an idea for a film, mapping it out in his mind, as it were. I was a little hurt, to be honest. But I understand that the creative process is a very delicate dance. Ford is a genius. I'd seen all of his films before we'd ever even met, and I always found them — searing. Just searing and penetrating in a very powerful way. So, I didn't want to question his process. It's very important that an artist be nurtured...So he went out. And I took a shower. This was about noon. After that, I tried to do some writing. I'm a poet — vocationally. That's what I do. I was working on a new poem: "Untitled 103," and I was very absorbed in the poem. It's about wind. Wind as a metaphor for God as a force in our lives. Or the lack thereof. The stillness, the arbitrariness of a random world. And the work was going very well. I was really just vomiting images like spoiled sushi (That may be an ill-considered metaphor, but you get my gist.) I was absorbed and productive.

I'd written — three lines, I think, when I looked at the clock and it was ten thirty. This happens sometimes, when I'm writing. It's as if I fall into a hole in the time-space continuum. I am pulled — I've strayed.

So it's ten-thirty and I haven't heard from Ford. But I didn't worry. I was unfamiliar with his process and it seemed possible that he'd been out walking for *ten and a half hours.* So I tried to go to sleep. But I couldn't sleep! I tossed and turned. I had visions in my head of Ford in a hospital, or dead in a ditch, the victim of wandering thugs. And then, of course, I started thinking … nothing happened to him! He hates me. He's gone. We rushed into this and now he's left me. It's over. I did something wrong. I was too aggressive! Or too passive! Or too passive-aggressive! I went into a shame spiral! And I cried, and I cursed and I prayed to God that this was a terrible dream, and that any minute I'd wake up and Ford'd be lying next to me!

And then the phone rang — thank God! I looked at the clock: six-fifteen. It was Ford! I was so relieved! "FORD! WHERE ARE YOU!?" — I tried to keep the panic out of my voice. I didn't want to seem, for a minute, the over-bearing wife. He said he was fine. "I just need some time," he said. "I'm working on a film and I need some time."…. And then, he hung up. He hung up. And haven't heard from him since. *(Pause.)* Bea? Bea? Are you still there?

BEA.   You're a poet? That's what you do for a living? You're a poet?

AMANDA.   Yes!

BEA.   What kind of living is that? Is there money in that? How do you —

AMANDA.   I have money. Money is not the issue!

BEA.   I never heard of such a thing.

AMANDA.   You've never heard of poetry?

BEA.   *(Insulted.)* I've heard of poetry! I'm not stupid. I never heard of anyone doing it for a living.

AMANDA.   Well, I did inherit some money, when I was

younger.

BEA.   Knew it!

AMANDA.   I have published many poems! I have a poem in this week's *New Yorker!*

BEA.   What's it called?

AMANDA.   Why do you ask?

BEA.   I'll pick it up. I'll take a look.

AMANDA.   "Untitled 94."

BEA.   I'll take a look.

AMANDA.   Don't bother.

BEA.   I'm very impressed. Tell me. How long did you know "Ford —" I just adore that name! How long did you know him before you got married?

AMANDA.   Why do you ask?

BEA.   How long?

AMANDA.   What difference does that make?

BEA.   Who's the professional here?

AMANDA.   Are you a psychologist?

BEA.   No. I am not.

AMANDA.   What kind of professional are you?

BEA.   I ran a needle-point store for *several* years.

AMANDA.   And that qualifies you —

BEA.   *(Insulted.)* We go through a very long, grueling, six-hour training process before we are allowed to man the phones!

AMANDA.   I see.

BEA.   Not just anyone can walk in off the street.

AMANDA.   I don't think a six-hour training process qualifies you —

BEA.   My life qualifies me!!

AMANDA.   And how is that?

BEA.   I am a survivor!

AMANDA.   But that you mean, you're old?

BEA.   *(A threat.)* I'm hanging up!

AMANDA.   I'm sorry.

BEA.   My life has not been easy! Judge me not lest you be judged young lady is what I think I mean. I've been in your place! I've known the misery of abandonment — why, when my husband died, I thought my world was coming to an end!

I never felt so all alone!

AMANDA. Do you have any children?

BEA. One, yes, but don't get me started. My husband's death just pulled the rug out from under me — didn't want to do a thing! I didn't want to wash or dress or go to the movies. Nothing. I just cried. I curled myself up into the fetal position and I cried. One day, honest to God, I found myself on the kitchen floor in yesterday's nightgown, curled up, like a snail, unable to move. That's the bottom. That, my dear, is the end! When you're snailed up on the kitchen floor. I just wanted to die! And I never even cared for my late husband.

AMANDA. Pardon me?

BEA. But. I pulled myself up, by my bootstraps and started over. I made a life for myself! So you want to know my qualifications? I've come back from the grave! That's my qualification!

AMANDA. I see.

BEA. So how long did you know him before?

AMANDA. *(After a hesitation.)* A month.

BEA. A month?

AMANDA. Two weeks.

BEA. You marry someone you know two weeks?

AMANDA. Yes!

BEA. Does that seem fool-hardy to you? It seems fool-hardy to me.

AMANDA. Well, hind-sight is always twenty-twenty, isn't it?

BEA. Don't be fresh. I'm just saying that that isn't very long —

AMANDA. I knew him a week!!! A week!!! All right?

BEA. How'd you meet?

AMANDA. We met at an installation.

BEA. What the hell is that? I don't know what that is?

AMANDA. An exhibit. We met at an art show by my friend, Tipper Bousché.

BEA. This is a name?

AMANDA. It is, yes. I'd been dating Cowel Selig, the performance artist. Maybe you've —

BEA. No.

AMANDA. Well, that was over.

BEA. How'd it end?

AMANDA. He killed himself.

BEA. Was that last Tuesday, or Wednesday, or something?

AMANDA. *Months* ago.

BEA. Then it wasn't my fault.

AMANDA. He died on stage: self-immolated. It was part of his performance.

BEA. My.

AMANDA. It was very well reviewed.

BEA. I prefer a musical.

AMANDA. I assume.

BEA. Did you see *Blood Brothers?*

AMANDA. No — in any event, I went with Binky to the gallery and met Ford.

BEA. And?

AMANDA. And I was very attracted to him. He is — very attractive. He has very beautiful eyes. And beautiful hair. And hands. Simply wonderful hands.

BEA. Yeah, yeah, he has hands. What happened?

AMANDA. Eventually, we came back here.

BEA. Your place?

AMANDA. Yes.

BEA. What was wrong with his place?

AMANDA. He was staying with friends. So we came back here. And, of course, we'd both been drinking a bit. I wouldn't say we were drunk, but we'd had some drinks. He said he'd like to hear some poems.

BEA. Very, very smooth. *(As Amanda speaks, Bea's light slowly dims.)*

AMANDA. And so I read him some poems. I read him "Untitled 24," and "Untitled 87," and one I hadn't titled yet at all. He listened. We looked out the window, and from my apartment, one can see into the building across the street. It seemed that everyone was home. There were lights in all the windows. And in each apartment, I know this sounds far-fetched, but in each apartment there was someone watching television. Every window was a painting of isolation. Every tele-

15

vision reflected blue, onto a solitary face. And somehow, the power of that sight filled me, with a huge sorrow — I wrote a poem about it later: "Untitled 106." — I was overwhelmed with a mammoth despair.... I started to cry. And Ford said nothing. He understood. I didn't need to explain; he felt it as well. And he comforted me, without words He touched his lips to my tears and traced his hand, so lightly, on the side of my face, touching my cheek and jaw, then neck ... he smelled of white wine and his own body. I felt his lips on my ear and I shut my eyes as he unbuttoned my blouse. He put his mouth on my nipples and I was no longer crying. Or thinking. He shed his shirt, so I could feel his skin as I stepped out of my skirt. Our clothes blew, crazy down the block as he kissed my stomach. I took his head in my hands, and looked at him and his face was very beautiful to me, so I kissed him and put my tongue in his mouth, which tasted wonderful, and he held me from behind, with one hand, while he slid the other between my legs and into me, where I was wet and wanted him to be. He was smiling, like a bad child, as we simply, had each other, again, and again. Until it was morning. *(A long pause. Bea's light returns revealing that she has been deeply effected by the sexual content of Amanda's story. Bea breaths deeply, her hand on her chest.)* Of course later, I realized that if I could see them, my neighbors could, naturally, see me and now I feel compelled to wear dark glasses whenever I put out my garbage.

BEA. That was ... very ... well, there are no words.

AMANDA. It was wonderful.

BEA. So ... you had an orgasm?

AMANDA. *(Of course.)* Yes.

BEA. I never.

AMANDA. Oh?

BEA. I never much cared for it.

AMANDA. I'm so sorry.

BEA. My late husband was not an attractive person.

AMANDA. I'm sure he had fine qualities.

BEA. And that's where you'd be wrong.

AMANDA. Oh.

16

BEA. He had hair coming outa places you cannot imagine.

AMANDA. And yet you were devastated when he died.

BEA. Well, as for company, he was better than a book.

AMANDA. Now you have your children.

BEA. One. Child. But don't get me going. A *meeskite.*

AMANDA. A what?

BEA. An ugly thing. A sad thing. Pathetic.

AMANDA. That's too bad.

BEA. So. The two of you met and fucked on the first date. What happened next?

AMANDA. Well, the next day, we did, actually, talk. We got to know each other and found we had an enormous number of things in common.

BEA. Such as? List please.

AMANDA. Well, we're both intense Fassbinder fans.

BEA. Uh-huh.

AMANDA. And we both had rather unpleasant childhoods.

BEA. How so? Elucidate.

AMANDA. *(Irritated.)* I don't want to go into it. I don't see how it's pertinent.

BEA. *(Insulted.)* Fine.

AMANDA. So we were in bed for several days —

BEA. Does no one in your social circle have a job?

AMANDA. We have jobs!! We write!! We're artists! We make art. That's our job. People think if you don't make a shoe, or, or a desk, or something tangible that you're not worth any-thing. We make something for the soul, something for the spirit. Is that not tangible enough for you? Your attitude is just symbolic of everything that's wrong with people today.

BEA. I asked a question.

AMANDA. A question heavy with the Sisyphusian burden of judgment.

BEA. Excuse me.

AMANDA. Where was I?

BEA. In bed.

AMANDA. And I suggested that we should spend the rest of our lives together.

BEA. And he said?

17

AMANDA. He ... smiled. He agreed. We were married by my friend Caitlin's brother. It was lovely. We wrote our own vows. I, of course, wrote a poem. Ford read from *Tess of the D'Urbervilles* — I have no idea why. And then we were off to Martha's Vineyard and now he's gone and I don't know what I'm going to do!!

BEA. What've you been doing?

AMANDA. Waiting. Waiting and waiting, as women have always done since Miss Havisham's wedding dress got covered in cobwebs.

BEA. Have you seen anyone?

AMANDA. You mean professionally? Is that what you mean?

BEA. I mean socially. A friend. Friends are very important. When my late husband keeled, I woulda dropped dead if it wasn't for my friend Thelma, a lovely human being, who picked me up with a ladle.

AMANDA. Well, I haven't. I mean I planned to. I was supposed to see — I was on my way to visit my friend, Binky, this morning. But I never made it.

BEA. What happened? *(As Amanda tells her story Bea's light dims again. Amanda's lighting should reflect both her emotional state and the facts of the story. As she speaks we get further and further into her mind.)*

AMANDA. Well, I left my apartment. It was about noon and it was a nice day, so I thought I'd walk to her house. She lives on 75th and Columbus, which, I realize, is a very long walk, but I thought the exercise would do me good — I hadn't eaten anything yet, so I stopped at the diner on my corner, for some breakfast, and I picked up a newspaper so I'd have something to do.

I was reading my paper when the waiter came over and asked if I was ... *alone.* Well! It was obvious that I was *alone!* I was sitting there, in a booth, by myself — did he think I thought I had an imaginary friend with me?! I was *alone!* Did he have to rub it in? Was he trying to be funny? Did he think he was, in some way, better than me? It was in his tone. He said, "Are you alone?" But what he meant to say was, "You're alone. *Aren't you!?*" — And I can't imagine that he's not alone every single day of his miserable, *pathetic* life! He has terrible skin. And it's not attractive. Not the way bad skin, or at least the remnants of bad skin, is attractive on some people. On some men!! It's never attractive on women — have you noticed that? Just one more example of the injustices we are forced to suffer! If we have bad skin, we're grotesque! Let a man have bad skin and he can be Richard Burton for God's sake! I HATE BEING A WOMAN!!

I've strayed.

The point is this waiter has terrible skin, and greasy hair and his breath stinks of something dead and his face is entirely too close to mine, and he insults me with his breath and his tone of voice and asks if I'm alone. I feel my face go flush and I want to rip his head off! I'd *like* to pull his hair out, only I'd never be able to get a decent grip — it looks as if it hasn't been washed in a decade! I want to pick up my butter knife and stab in his sunken, caved-in chest! But! I simply respond, *(Grandly:)*

"No, I'm married, thank you." *(Pause.)*

I realize, now, of course, that my answer was illogical. I realize that it was inappropriate. But, at the time, it was all I could think to say.

Well, he leans back and, really, in the most supercilious manner, he leers at me and intones, "I meant, are you *eating* alone." "I KNEW WHAT YOU MEANT!" I KNEW WHAT HE MEANT! I don't know why I said what I said, I just said it! He made me sick. I hope he dies. I shouted, "I KNEW WHAT YOU MEANT!" And I am not a person who shouts, generally. I don't like shouting. It hurts to shout and it hurts to be shouted at. My mother shouted quite a bit and I always thought the veins in her neck looked like the roots of a tree. But I shouted. Everyone looked at me ... because I was standing. I didn't mean to be standing. I didn't remember standing, but I was. I was standing. I must've leapt up when I shouted. So I was standing and everyone was staring at me. The place was very crowded, much more crowded than I ever recall seeing it before. And suddenly, it occurred to me, that these *people, my neighbors,* gawking at me in endless silence,

19

were the very same people who had watched Ford and myself have sex that first night when we met. I was so humiliated! I thought I would die! Or be sick! I was certain I was going to be sick right there at my table, standing up, being stared at! And then everyone in the neighborhood would mutter under their breath, every time they saw me, "Oh there goes that woman. We've seen her have sex, and we've seen her vomit."

I WOULD LIKE, AT SOME POINT IN MY LIFE, TO CLING, WITH WHATEVER ENERGY I HAVE, TO MY DIGNITY! What have we got but our dignity? Women are worthless in this world! Every aspect of our culture conspires to keep us subjugated under the oppressive thumb of the beauty myth. If you're attractive, congratulations! Because you own it all! You run the world! But God forbid you should have bad skin, or gain a pound or lose a leg or be, in any way, a deviant, from what the power-brokers and the plutocrats and politicians and the magazines and the television and the government and the OIL COMPANIES, WHICH OWN ALL THE OTHER STUFF TO BEGIN WITH — God forbid you should deviate from what the president of Shell Oil decides is attractive and YOU ARE A DISPOSABLE HUMAN BEING! YOU ARE A DEAD BIRD ON THE HIGHWAY! — Not that I'm unattractive, mind you! I am very attractive. I know I am!

But I wasn't feeling very attractive this morning while I was being stared at by the same nasty, judgmental, *narrow* swine who got their rocks off watching me HAVE SEX! I just stood there in that diner, for what seemed like hours, and then, with all the composure and dignity I could muster, which was considerable, I said, "I've changed my mind!" And I left. *(A long pause.)*

I was all the way on forty-third street before I realized that I'd left my purse. *(Pause; her frenzy returns at once.)*

There's another example of how we are kept under the thumb of a patriarchal culture!! PURSES! Do men have purses? No! They have pockets! Why don't we have pockets?! I'll tell you why, because they would make our hips bulge! It might make our buttocks look lumpy! And we couldn't have that!! No! So we have purses! And you can either get a dainty, little purse that you have to hold in your hand, in which case you live your whole life with only one hand available, giving the world a head start on beating you with, literally, one hand tied behind your back!! Or you can get one of those big old shoulder bags which hurt like hell and leave deep red welts on your skin and I'm certain it throws your spine out of alignment, so you end up in a panic about getting osteoporosis. And you spend all your time worrying and your money on calcium supplements, WHICH DO NO GOOD ANYWAY, BECAUSE YOU JUST KNOW YOU'LL END UP WITH A HUMP AND ALL YOUR DRESSES ARE GOING TO LOOK LONGER IN THE FRONT!! OF COURSE YOU CAN ALWAYS GET A KNAPSACK — BUT THEN, PEOPLE JUST THINK YOU'RE A LESBIAN!! I'D LIKE TO GET MY HANDS ON THE FILTHY, MISOGYNIST MOTHER-FUCKER — *I'D LIKE TO MURDER WHOMEVER THE PRICK WAS THAT INVENTED THE HANDBAG!!* (*She composes herself a bit.*)

I've strayed.

As I was saying, I was at Times Square when I realized that I'd forgotten my handbag. I start to feel a little dizzy. And nauseous. I hadn't had anything to eat. I haven't eaten in days — I don't like to keep any food in the house because it attracts roaches and I just end up eating it when I shouldn't. I hadn't been hungry all week. But all of a sudden I was *very* hungry, famished, starved! I wasn't sure if I could make it back to the diner on my corner without fainting. I had to eat something! I had sixteen cents in my pocket. So ... I loitered at a hot-dog stand. Now, I try not to eat hot-dogs because of the nitrites, but at this point they weren't hot-dogs, they were I.V.s! They were plasma! They were bread and water! AND THEY COST A DOLLAR TWENTY-FIVE!

I tried looking sweet and pathetic, like the poster for *Les Miserables:* I let a tear come to my eye and looked to heaven ... (*She does so.*)

But the man selling the hot dogs ignored me completely!

So I tried flirting with him. Subtly. I wet my lips and held my arms in a way that I thought accentuated my bust. *(She does so.)*

He smiled, at me, *lewdly,* and I saw that what few teeth he had in his head were the khaki color of dead leaves! I was dizzy and sick and swooning, but I wasn't ready to sell myself to this fetid extortionist for a dollar twenty-five's worth of pig snouts and feet!

I was sure there were other vendors, kinder souls who'd take pity on me ... and so I headed south! Back to my corner, back to the diner, back to the hateful waiter and my purse. At first I kept my eyes on the pavement, searching all the while for a nickel, a dime — a subway token I could barter.... Then I noticed ... my hand was out, in front of me ... my palm was up. I wasn't begging, per se. But if someone *wanted* to give me their spare change, who am I not to help them purge their guilt?! FORD DID THIS TO ME! HE REDUCED ME TO THIS! I HATE HIM!

But I did my best: groveling, begging, looking wan — but the competition was fierce! I was surrounded, on all sides, by people so disfigured by their misfortune I was certain I'd stumbled onto the set of a Fellini film! A woman on my right had no shoes. I felt badly for her, until I realized that a man on my left had no feet! He was chasing me on a skateboard, spitting and shouting at me in a language I didn't recognize — but I gather I'd been working his turf — so I ran. I ran ahead, the traffic swimming in front of me! I no longer wanted to eat! I didn't want to see Binky! I wanted my purse! And my key! And my bed! And a bath! I ran forward! Every block I survived was a victory! And then I made it!

It was across the street.... Home!... I was standing on the corner, surrounded by what seemed to be hundreds of children all wild and loud and out of control, and under the care of ONE adult with a badge from The Chelsea Day School. The sun was so hot! I was sure I was standing under an enormous magnifying glass! And soot from the cars and buses was making me sicker and sicker! And we were all together, standing on the corner, waiting for the light to change. AND IT WOULDN'T! It would not! We stood for hours! We waited weeks and the fucking light WOULD NOT CHANGE! And then ... it turned green — I KNOW IT TURNED GREEN! I KNOW IT! So I staggered, or stumbled or walked into the street and a car, FROM NOWHERE, came zooming at me! It was headed directly at me!! It was going to kill me!! I WAS GOING TO DIE!

It swerved! It swerved to the side! Onto the curb and all at once the children were screaming! SCREAMING! But I didn't look back! I RAN! I couldn't turn around! I RAN! Past the diner!! I don't know what happened! I DON'T WANT TO KNOW WHAT HAPPENED! I RAN! STRAIGHT TO MY BUILDING AND HOME! *(Bea's light returns.)*

BEA. *(Simply.)* What do you think happened?

AMANDA. I don't know.

BEA. You think someone was hit?

AMANDA. I said, I don't know! I didn't look.

BEA. Was it on the news?

AMANDA. *(With great bitterness.)* That light was green! I didn't do anything wrong! I wasn't driving the goddamn car! I didn't do anything!

BEA. Maybe nothing happened.

AMANDA. I do not want to talk about this! This is not why I called you! My husband is gone and I haven't eaten in a week and I don't have a purse and THIS IS NOT WHY I CALLED YOU! YOU ARE NOT HELPING ME! *(A long pause. General lighting has returned, but it is a good deal dimmer.)*

BEA. What are you wearing?

AMANDA. What? Why do you ask?

BEA. Answer the question.

AMANDA. A tee shirt.

BEA. Change your clothes.

AMANDA. My life is in a shambles and —

BEA. Change your clothes!

AMANDA. I fail to see how that —

BEA. You have a shorty nightgown?

AMANDA. Yes.

BEA. Put it on.

AMANDA. No.

23

BEA.   Do what I'm telling you.

AMANDA.   I don't want to.

BEA.   Put. It. On.

AMANDA.   What are you talking about?

BEA.   Everything looks one hundred percent better from inside a shorty nightgown.

AMANDA.   *(Ironic.)* That is very, very wise.

BEA.   Listen to me. He'll be back.

AMANDA.   Who cares? Who cares? I don't care any more..

BEA.   You fancy yourself some modern woman. But you know, things don't change. Some things are forever. The food chain is as it always was. Men rule the world. *But* penises rule men! And who rules the penises? We do, darling. People panic. People do things. But he'll be back. And when he comes back, not one word out of you! You hear me? Don't ask him where he's been. Act like nothing happened.

AMANDA.   You're insane.

BEA.   I will not tolerate rudeness!... Let me tell you, when I married my late husband, I was pregnant — not with his kid, but I was pregnant. I was very good-looking when I was younger. But the father wasn't Jewish, so I decided — or actually, my mother decided, it wouldn't go. So I married what'shisname, my dead husband. I'll never forget waking up, in Atlantic City, the day after. I'm wide awake, staring at this fat lump of hairy nothing that I married, and, let me tell you, if I coulda run, I woulda. But I was going to have a child. So, instead, I just pulled the hair on his back as hard as I could. You see my point? *(A key turns in the door.)*

AMANDA.   Shut up!

BEA.   I will not tolerate —

AMANDA.   Someone's at the door! *(Bea disappears. The door opens, revealing Ford. He and Amanda stand, just looking at each other for a moment.)* Ford.... Where've you been?

BEA.   *(On the speaker phone.)* I told ya not to ask him that! *(Amanda hangs up the phone.)*

AMANDA.   *(After a pause.)* I mean it doesn't really matter where you've been, does it? You've been working on a film. I understand. I know that the creative process is a very delicate flower. And you've been working. Haven't you? *(Ford sits. He is deep in thought and deeply troubled. He has something to say, but it is very difficult for him. He puts his head in his hands for a moment, and agonizes.)*

FORD. Well —

AMANDA. I drove you away! Didn't I? We shouldn't've gotten married. It was a bad idea. I'm sorry. It was my idea and you felt cornered, or something. Is that it? Do you want to talk about it? Is that it?... Are you tired? We can talk tomorrow. That's fine. You're probably tired. We can talk tomorrow after a good night's sleep. *(Ford rises, looks at her and starts to head for the bedroom.)*

We do love each other though, don't we? I love you and you love me, so we love each other. *(Ford stops. He turns and looks at her.)*

You're in love with someone else, aren't you! I can tell. *(Ford moves towards her, reaching out.)*

I'm babbling. I realize I'm babbling. I find that I'm babbling. But you see, I've been cooped-up here lately — not that I didn't go out, while you were gone. I did. But not much. *(He looks away.)*

Is there someone else? Perhaps we rushed into this a bit too quickly. But then, perhaps we didn't. Time'll tell. Would you like something to eat? Are you hungry? We don't have any food — but we could order something ... if you have a credit card. I've lost my purse. *(He sits again and struggles to find the words to say what he must. He looks around the room, scratches his head, takes a deep breath and just as he is about to speak, she cuts him off.)*

YOU THINK I'M UGLY, DON'T YOU? TELL ME, WHAT PART OF ME DO YOU THINK IS UGLIEST? *(He rises to protest. She cuts him off.)*

I know I'm beautiful. You're right. I'm a beautiful woman. I wasn't always. When I was a child, I was painfully fat. Did you know that? *(He shakes his head and sits.)*

I never mentioned that. Did you ever wonder why there are no pictures around here, of me? Before I turned twenty?

25

Did you think I was a vampire? Did you think I had a Nosferatu childhood? *(He shrugs.)*

When I was twenty, I went on a diet. I fasted for three weeks. I lost forty-five pounds. I dieted all summer and when I went back to school I told everyone I was my own cousin. Isn't that something? — YOU MAKE ME FEEL SO FAT! *(He puts his head in his hands.)*

Everyone believed I was my own cousin. That was the summer my mother died. We had a house on The Cape. We went to the beach one day and she drowned. She went out into the ocean and swam and swam and I never saw her again. Maybe she swam to France and became a chanteuse. I changed my name to Amanda that summer. *(He looks up, surprised.)*

Between my sophomore and junior years at Sarah Lawrence. Betty was a fat girl who's only friends were society's cast-offs. Amanda had no more friends than Betty, but people assumed it was by choice. — Is it someone I know? The person you've found? *(He rises again, about to speak. She cuts him off.)*

I can be Betty again, if you'd prefer that. My mother used to say you can be whatever you want. She meant, you can be WHOMever you want. Everyone said she drowned. They said it was an accident. My father said, "Things happen." I think she killed herself. I think she wanted to die. Maybe we should talk tomorrow. *(He starts to exit.)*

While you were gone, I did some work! *(He turns to her.)*

I've been writing as well. I wrote a new poem. I did. It's very unusual — for me. This poem. I call it — well, I don't have a name for it yet. But it's a narrative poem, and well, it's about this man. And he's very attractive and very ... loved. And one day, he finds himself married. And he loves his wife and she loves him, but he feels ... confined, I think is the word I used. Maybe it was trapped. I can't remember. You see he's an artist and he's very, very sensitive. *(She is near tears.)*

And he wants to get away, but he knows this will just ... kill her. The wife. This will destroy her, for reasons that are absolutely not his fault. But that's the way it is. And she simply wants to kill him. *(He moves towards her.)*

But instead, she just looks at him. *(She moves towards him.)*
And she touches his face. *(She does this, sweetly.)*
And she runs her fingers along his lips. *(She does this.)*
And she looks in his eyes ... because she loves him. And she takes him in her hand. *(She places her hand on his crotch.)* And she strokes him. *(She massages his genitalia through his trousers. His breathing deepens.)*
And she kisses him. *(They kiss. It is very passionate and sexual.)*

FADEOUT

SCENE 2

OTTO

The middle of the night. The lights come up on the chic studio apartment of Serge Stubin, a handsome, trim man of 30. There is a soloflex, a huge closet and a large bed. Serge is lounging on the bed, listening to music, wearing trendy, bike-short style underpants. After a moment, there is a knock at the door. Serge rises, turns off the CD and goes to the door.

SERGE. Who is it?

OTTO. *(Offstage.)* It's me.

SERGE. *(Disappointed, irritated.)* Me who?

OTTO. *(Offstage.)* Me, the one true love of your life.

SERGE. *(Returning to the bed.)* Go away, Otto.

OTTO. *(Offstage.)* Let me in!

SERGE. It's the middle of the night.

OTTO. *(Offstage.)* Serge! I'm being followed!

SERGE. Consider it flattery.

OTTO. *(Offstage.)* Let me in!

SERGE. Go home!

OTTO. *(Offstage.)* Today's my birthday. I'm thirty-four years old today.

SERGE. Today is not your birthday.

OTTO. *(Offstage.)* Yesterday was my birthday?

SERGE. Go away. Go.

OTTO. *(Offstage.)* Let me in, or I'll kill myself! I mean it. I'll do it right here on the doorstep! How'll that look? How'd you like that? Well? I mean it! I'll do it! *(Pause.)* LET ME IN!! *(Serge goes wearily to the door, and opens it, revealing Otto, a wildly over-weight man carrying a bag of groceries.)*

SERGE. What do you want?

OTTO. I got fired.

SERGE. I'm sorry.

OTTO. I want to see you.

SERGE. You can't come in. I'm expecting someone.

OTTO. I won't stay long. I promise. *(Otto forces his way in. He makes himself at home quickly unpacking groceries, starting with doughnuts. He eats as he talks.)* It's *unbelievably* hot in here! Is the air conditioning broken? I'm sweating already. You look well, but then you always look well. How've you been? I saw a picture of someone who looked just like you in a magazine. It was Honcho. I cut the penis out of the picture.

SERGE. What are you doing here?!

OTTO. I got fired —

SERGE. So you said.

OTTO. That job was everything to me! I have nothing! I *am* nothing! I'm a fat, middle-aged man with nothing to look forward to but the embrace of death.

SERGE. You're thirty-three.

OTTO. Please! With my cholesterol and my blood sugar, I'll never make sixty. This is the twilight of my life. I'm alone and jobless in my declining years.

SERGE. What happened?

OTTO. They said I wasn't funny anymore. How funny do you have to be to introduce a bunch of *no-talents?* They said I'd lost my *joie de vivre!* Of course, I've lost my *joie de vivre* — I'm fat, I'm lonely, I have a new pimple, I'm thirty-six —

SERGE. You're thirty-three!

OTTO. And I'm still getting pimples! Who could be funny under the circumstances?

SERGE. You're getting crumbs on the bed!

OTTO. Isn't that cute? Isn't that sweet? It's just like the old days. Remember how you used to scream at me when I ate in the bed? You'd scream with such rage, you turned purple. I was so happy. It can be like that again.

SERGE. It will be, if you don't —

OTTO. Do you want one?

SERGE. No.

OTTO. They're delicious! — It's hot as a pizza house in here. Are you growing pot or something?

SERGE. I like it warm.

OTTO. I'm just going to turn this up. *(Otto adjusts the ther-*

mostat.) Who needs them anyway?!! I survived before that crummy little nightclub and I'll survive without it! I'm not a comic. I'm an actor! I did Chekhov and Inge! It was only college, true, but I have training! I have technique! — That was the best job I ever had! Steady work, a steady paycheck, four nights a week and I could live off it! And it was so easy! What am I going to do?

SERGE.   You'll get another job.

OTTO.   Oh you don't care!! You never cared! You only care about you! You're self-centered, that's your problem — Are those Calvin Klein? They're cute. — You know what this means, don't you? It's back to the notions counter for me!

SERGE.   You worked at Barneys in European suits.

OTTO.   I just want to die!

SERGE.   Well you can't die here. Not tonight.

OTTO.   Do you think I made it too cold? Can I stay? Can I stay over? Can I sleep here tonight?

SERGE.   Of course not.

OTTO.   Please?

SERGE.   I told you, someone's coming over.

OTTO.   I don't believe you. I think you're lying. Who'd come over at this hour? Only an insane person, present company excluded, of course. I think you're lying. You lie with every breath. You're a liar, that's your problem.

SERGE.   Go home. Get some sleep.

OTTO.   *(Lying.)* I can't. My house burned down.

SERGE.   What are you talking about?

OTTO.   It did. It burned to the ground. It's a miracle no one was killed. I think someone set it. That's what I think. I think the management company did it for the insurance. That sounds possible, doesn't it?

SERGE.   No.

OTTO.   You're too cynical, *that's* your problem. *(The phone rings. As Serge answers it, Otto removes a package of pretzel rods from his sack. He takes one and stacks doughnuts on it. He then eats this creation as if it were an ear of corn.)*

SERGE.   *(Into the phone.)* Hello.... Oh, yes, I'm fine.... No, it's not too late.... Oh.... Oh.... Oh. That is too bad. *(He ex-*

tends the phone to Otto.) It's for you.

OTTO. *(Taking the phone.)* Oh. I left this number on my machine. *(Into the phone:)* Hello?... Why are you calling me here?... Serge is fine.... No. No.... No, this does NOT mean we're back together.... Well, *I* visit people in the middle of the night ... I'm sorry ... I'm sorry ... I'm sorry.... I've got to go ... I've got to go ... I've got to go. *(He hangs up.)* It was my mother.

SERGE. You've got to go.

OTTO. She thinks I'm going to kill myself or something. She thinks I'm taking this job thing too hard. My analyst says I was overly involved in my work. My analyst says I've been looking for the wrong kind of fulfillment. My analyst makes me sick. Do you want a pretzel?

SERGE. No.

OTTO. Do you think you could ever love me again?

SERGE. No.

OTTO. Don't toy with me. Don't tease me along.

SERGE. I said no.

OTTO. Just tell me the truth. Just lay it on the line. I'm a grown-up. I can take it. Be honest. You shilly-shally, *that's* your problem.

SERGE. I'm in love with someone else.

OTTO. I remember the first time I saw you. In Barney's. You were spectacular looking, to me a any rate. Not that you're not good-looking, I don't mean that. But some people don't think you're as good-looking as me. I mean as I do. Everyone things you're better looking than I am. Even *my mother* thinks you're better looking than me. Did you know she shows your picture to people? People ask her if she has a son and she shows them your picture. You've made her very proud.

SERGE. Is there no way to stop you?

OTTO. I certainly hope not. Obviously you're good-looking. You're a model. You have to be good-looking to be a model. But then again, you only do runway. You're not good-looking enough for print, are you? Is it chilly in here now? You could love me again, if I were thin.

SERGE. I doubt that.

31

OTTO. Oh, you may not think so, but I know it. I'm sure of it. I'm on a diet. I've lost eighty-five pounds. Can you tell? Do I look thinner?

SERGE. No.

OTTO. Well, actually, I gained four pounds. But I don't think four pounds really shows up. I know in the past, when I've lost four pounds, it didn't show. When was that? As I was saying, before I was so *rudely* interrupted, I'm on a new diet. I have a Slimfast shake with every meal. Have you tried Slimfast?

SERGE. Of course not.

OTTO. You're afraid to try new things, *that's* your problem. I like you're hair. Are you combing it differently, or at all? Slimfast is delicious! It goes fabulously with pretzels! *(He pulls a can of Slim-Fast out of his bag.)* I'm not thirsty yet. Maybe later — You'd love me again, if I was thinner. I told my analyst that I was going to come and see you, and you know what she did? She laughed! She burst into gales of laughter! She told me she was crying. She cries all the time. I don't think she's happy. I think she's got serious problems. Would you love me again if I weighed a hundred pounds? Would you love me if I weighed fifty pounds? Would you love me if I looked like one of those living corpses in the photographs from the liberation of Auschwitz?

SERGE. I can't say I'd love you. I might prefer you.

OTTO. So tell me, what've you been doing with yourself lately? I'm fascinated.

SERGE. I did the Gaultier show and Anna Sui menswear.

OTTO. Runway modeling must be soooo stimulating. Such a challenge.

SERGE. It's fine. It's easy.

OTTO. Tell me, do you ever worry that you'll fall off the ramp? D'you ever worry that you'll swagger, blindly, off the runway and into the lap of the editor from *GQ*?

SERGE. No!

OTTO. D'you ever worry that you'll put the clothes on upside down? D'you ever traipse down the catwalk with your arms in the leg holes and the pants wrapped around your back, like a bolero jacket?

SERGE.   I like what I do! The money is good. The people are nice.

OTTO.   I bet they are. Why shouldn't they be? — It is definitely freezing in here now. *(He adjusts the thermostat.)* What have they got to be bitter about? All those stunning young boys with perfect chests and perfect hair. They all have squares on their stomachs and perfect little geometric rear-ends. I'm a total failure! I'm washed up at thirty-eight!

SERGE.   You're thirty-three!!

OTTO.   Must you be correct all the time? What is this neurotic compulsion you have to be correct? You have a fetish, *that's* your problem.

SERGE.   I don't want to hurt your feelings —

OTTO.   *(Pulling a pack of Yodels from his bag.)* Do you like Yodels? Probably not. I've always loved Yodels. When I was a kid I used to unroll them and eat them like a piece of pizza. It made them seem like more. My analyst says my parents never paid enough attention to me, so I have a neurotic fear of there never being enough of anything. I don't know what she's talking about most of the time. *(Otto shoves a whole Yodel into his mouth.)*

SERGE.   How often are you seeing her? *(Otto chews, savoring his food for a moment. Then, cheerfully:)*

OTTO.   Twice a day. Remember how happy we were?

SERGE.   I don't remember that we were particularly happy.

OTTO.   You reinvent history, *that's* your problem. We were in an advanced state of bliss! My living here with you was the happiest two years of my life.

SERGE.   Two years?!

OTTO.   Did I say two years? I meant four years. It just flew by in half the time.

SERGE.   You never lived here!

OTTO.   Time flies when you're in love.

SERGE.   We dated for a couple of weeks!

OTTO.   You must've had it awful bad.

SERGE.   GET OUT!!

OTTO.   *(Sprawling on the bed.)* I loved this bed! I adored it!

It was ecstasy like death! You know that Jacques Brel song? "My death waits in a double bed —" The contortions, the experiments, the complete savage abandon!! If this bed could talk, the stories it could tell! — Is this the same bed? It smells different. Did you get a new bed?

SERGE.   I'm asking you nicely. I've tried to be direct. I've tried to be blunt. Now, I'm asking you as a friend —

OTTO.   We are friends, aren't we?

SERGE.   I suppose.

OTTO.   Then tell me, as a friend, what's wrong with me?

SERGE.   You're insane.

OTTO.   I'm forty years old and I have no one in my life!!

SERGE.   You are THIRTY-THREE!!

OTTO.   You have a terrible temper. You know that? I'm forty-one and you're twenty-eight, but with your temper and too much exercise, we'll be the same age in six months. *(The phone rings. Serge answers it.)*

SERGE.   Hello?... Yes ... yes ... yes ... yes. *(He extends the phone to Otto.)* It's for you.

OTTO.   *(Singing.)* I'm Mr. Popular! *(He takes the phone.)* Hello?... Obviously, I'm still here.... No, we're NOT back together yet!... No, no, I'm not making a fool of myself.... Yes, I saw her today.... She laughed.... Fifty dollars.... I have to go ... I'm hanging up! *(He hangs up.)* It was my mother.

SERGE.   Please leave.

OTTO.   She's lonely. She threw out her back. She's in traction.

SERGE.   We all have our problems.

OTTO.   *(Sarcastic.)* Oh you are so sympathetic. You're a saint! When you look up sympathy in the dictionary, it says, "see Serge Stubin." You're too good, that's your problem.

SERGE.   I'm sorry.

OTTO.   Oh, no. What do you care? The poor woman is stuck in a hospital bed somewhere, out in the night, her limbs hanging like a Calder mobile. Her son's out of work, wandering the streets, a forty-four-year-old nebbish with no future, and not much of past to speak of.

SERGE.   How did it happen?

34

OTTO.   Who cares! Who cares how it happened. I HATE
HER! SHE RUINED MY LIFE. THAT BITCH CONDEMNED
ME TO AN ETERNITY OF SELF-LOATHING. Did you know
I have a neurotic fear of being upside down? My analyst says
I need to experience my rage. She doodles while I talk to her.
She pretends to take notes, but I caught her one day. She was
drawing the Lincoln Memorial on a cocktail napkin! It was
very good, but I told her it stunk — I'm not giving her any
satisfaction — *(He pulls a box of Sno-Caps from his bag.)* I LOVE
SNO-CAPS!! Most people only eat them at the movies, but you
know they're good any time.
SERGE.   Don't eat any more.
OTTO.   *(Eating Sno-Caps.)* I'M STARVING! Did I mention that
I lie in bed at night and pretend you're there next to me? I
do. Did I mention that I hung your picture in my bathroom?
I taped it on the medicine chest, over the mirror. Now when
I wake up and I look at myself — I'm you!! I thought it would
make me like myself more. It didn't. It made me like you
more — and I cut myself shaving continually.
SERGE.   You have got to move on with your life.
OTTO.   I put two candles in the bathroom. One on either
side of your picture. It's like a shrine. Well it's not like a
shrine, it IS a shrine! I sacrifice small animals to you. I use
the sink. It's not as messy as you might imagine. I do mice,
and squirrels. Last week I did a baby goat.
SERGE.   Oh my God.
OTTO.   I'm lying. Or kidding. I don't know which — about
the goat.
SERGE.   Still.
OTTO.   And the mice. I killed a mosquito once. But it had
nothing to do with you. Do you remember how terrified you
were of bugs?
SERGE.   *You're* afraid of bugs.
OTTO.   You project, that's your problem. You always had a
neurotic fear of insects. I love them! I adore bugs. I keep
roaches as pets.
SERGE.   *(Pointing to a spot on the floor.)* Good. Then you can
have that one, there.

OTTO.   *(In terror.)* WHERE!? WHERE!? KILL IT! KILL IT
NOW!!
SERGE.   I'm lying. Or kidding. I don't know which.
OTTO.   I knew that. You are a complete sadist. You get plea-
sure from my abject misery. Maybe that's why I love you so
much. You could love me again if I were blonde. I could be
blonde. All those boys you work with are blonde, aren't they?
Except for the brunettes and the redheads. I could be blonde!
I could bleach my hair. I'd look repulsive. I'd look hideous.
You'd like that. You'd like it if I were freakishly ugly — Is it
unbelievably hot in here again? *(Otto goes to the thermostat.)*
SERGE.   You're going to break that!
OTTO.   OH WHAT DO YOU CARE? YOU CAN ALWAYS
BUY ANOTHER. You can buy anything you want. You have
all the money in the world and I am not speaking hyperboli-
cally. I think you do. I think you've used it all up. That's why
I can't ever seem to get any: YOU HAVE IT ALL!!! *(Otto throws
open Serge's closet, which is lined with mirrors. Upon seeing himself
he shrieks in horror and slams the doors shut.)* I love your apartment! It's so *put together.* Do you remember my apartment? It's
pathetic. Everything is old, and broken and chipped, from the
Salvation Army. I'm *forty-five years old* and I still have bookcases
made from cinder-blocks like a college dormitory.
SERGE.   You *have* money.
OTTO.   BLOOD MONEY! Money my father left me. I hated
him. He was a loathsome human being. Did I ever tell you
that I went to his funeral dressed as Bloody Mary? — The
character from *South Pacific,* not the cocktail. — I wore a gi-
ant moo-moo, a lei around my neck and a frozen daiquiri paper umbrella in my hair. I just did it to embarrass him. But
then no one came anyway. His was the most ill-attended funeral I've ever seen. And I've seen quite a few. Lately I go to
funerals just for the pick-me-up.
SERGE.   Why don't you take some of that money and go on
a trip?
OTTO.   I swore to myself I'd never spend one cent of the
filthy lucre that miserable old fart left me! He hated me! He
drank more than any two people I've ever known. The last

time I saw my father, you know what he said to me? Do you? He was in the hospital. He was on an iron lung. He was dying. Frito?

SERGE. No.

OTTO. He had a completely obsessive personality — pathetic. So he was in the hospital, clinging to life by his nicotine-yellow finger nails. And he's going on and on at me about my weight and being "light-in-the-loafers," which was the darling euphemism he used for "fairy." And his breathing was very labored — he had emphysema, or something. I can't remember. I never paid much attention. So he's on this iron lung, and his last words to me, the very last words he ever spoke: he reached out, red in the face, panic in his heart — he reached out and shrieked, "Otto! Otto! Please, no! Don't touch that plug!!"

SERGE. Oh my God!!

OTTO. But it was too late.

SERGE. You unplugged his iron lung?!

OTTO. His television! What's wrong with you?

SERGE. I thought —

OTTO. You thought I killed my father? You're insane, that's your problem. I unplugged his television. I went to visit him, I took time out of my busy schedule, which was completely empty as it happened, but he didn't know that! I went out of my way to visit that old gasbag and he has the nerve to lie there watching TV! He was the rudest person I ever knew. It was a football game, or something. I don't know. The one with the orange ball and hoops with nets. It was giving me a headache, so I unplugged it. And then he was angry — wouldn't say a word. He just lay there, like a corpse. It wasn't until later that I learned he had died. *(The phone rings.)*

SERGE. *(Weary.)* Go ahead.

OTTO. *(Into the phone.)* Hello?... Oh hello.... No, we're not back together yet!!... Yes, I realize that I'm a fat, ugly, lonely failure with nothing and no one in my life and that no one will shed a single tear when I die.... I'll talk to you later. *(He hangs up.)* It was my mother.

SERGE. I assumed.

OTTO.   Let's pretend we just met. OK? Let's pretend you picked me up in one of those bars you go to. I hate those places. Let's pretend. You be ... you! And I'll be me. OK? It'll be fun.

SERGE.   I don't want to.

OTTO.   You never want to have any fun, THAT'S your problem.

SERGE.   Look! I'VE EXPLAINED TO YOU —

OTTO.   I remember the first moment I saw you. How long ago was that? I can't remember now. Was it six months? Eight months?

SERGE.   It was FOUR years ago!

OTTO.   Was it? Was it really? Time stands still when I'm without you. Four years? How much did I weigh then?

SERGE.   Considerably less than you do now!

OTTO.   You're full of hate, baby! Hate just oozes out of you. Hate is gushing out of your skin. You wear hate the way the salesgirls in Bloomingdale's wear make-up. In heavy layers.

SERGE.   YOU'RE DRIVING ME CRAZY!

OTTO.   Did I mention that I tattooed your name on my buttocks? I did! It was extremely painful. It hurt like hell, but I did it! You know I have a neurotic fear of needles, but I tattooed your name on my rear end, in letters THREE feet tall!

SERGE.   Listen —

OTTO.   NOW I SIT ON YOU ALL THE TIME!

SERGE.   I HAVE TOLD YOU —

OTTO.   I know, I know. You're expecting someone!! Well, where is this mystery date? I don't see him. Let him come. I'll kill him! Then you, then myself — or any order you want. But you see, I don't think there is anyone coming over. I think you're lonely and bitter. I think every day since we split up has been as torturous for you as it has for me!

SERGE.   I'VE BEEN VERY HAPPY!

OTTO.   OH HIDE YOUR MISERY WITH LAUGHTER! YOU CAN'T FOOL ME. YOU'RE GRIEF STRICKEN TO THE POINT OF HYSTERIA, ONLY YOU HIDE IT WITH UNCOMMON PANACHE. I KNOW HOW BROKEN YOU'VE BEEN, BECAUSE I'VE BEEN THE SAME! THE DAYS ARE LONG,

BUT THE NIGHTS ARE LONGER! ADMIT YOU WANT ME
BACK! DON'T LET STUPID PRIDE STAND IN YOUR WAY.
WHAT'S THAT? SO SOONER THAN LATER YOU'LL BE A
ONCE-BEAUTIFUL, FADED, MALE-INGENUE TYPE,
WIZENED AND WITHERED ALONE WITH YOUR PRIDE.
WELL, LET ME TELL YOU PRIDE IS A COLD COMPANION
ON A BITTER WINTER'S NIGHT! I KNOW PRIDE! I KNOW
WHAT PRIDE IS! I HAVE NONE MYSELF, OF COURSE, BUT
I'VE SEEN IT IN OTHERS. FORGET YOUR PRIDE, LOVE
ME!!
SERGE.   For the last time, YOU HAVE GOT TO GET ON
WITH YOUR LIFE! Look at what you're doing to yourself!
You're killing yourself!
OTTO.   That'd make you happy, wouldn't it?
SERGE.   NO! No, Otto, it wouldn't. You can think what you
want. But I do not hate you. I don't. God knows why, but I
don't.
OTTO.   Is it hot in here? I'm having a sugar drop. *(Otto sits
on the floor and dumps out the remaining contents of his grocery bag.)*
SERGE.   I look at you and I remember what you used to be.
OTTO.   Before you destroyed me?
SERGE.   Before you ate yourself into this state!
OTTO.   Have I put on weight? Is that what you're saying? I
try not to get on the scale.
SERGE.   You were attractive.
OTTO.   I get vertigo from watching the dial spin, and spin,
and spin.
SERGE.   You were SANE! You were funny —
OTTO.   God, I'm hot.
SERGE.   I do not accept responsibility for you! I AM NOT
TO BLAME! *(Otto eats Oreo cookies rapidly, unscrewing them, scrap-
ing out the middle and throwing the cookie over his shoulder.)*
OTTO.   I can't imagine it's a question of blame.
SERGE.   It's been four years! Four long years! We dated
briefly. There was no passion. No great love! We dated briefly!
We never lived together! We never planned a future! WE!
DATED! BRIEFLY!
OTTO.   *(Offering.)* Would you like an Oreo?

SERGE. NO!!

OTTO. *(Coy.)* They're double stuff. *(Otto drinks a Yoo-hoo.)*

SERGE. WHAT IS WRONG WITH YOU!!? I thought this was over! I've held my breath! I've prayed! I've done good deeds! BUT NOTHING WORKED! YOU'RE BACK! I don't want to hurt you, but I need my peace! YOU HAVE GOT TO GET OVER ME! I'm no great catch to begin with, as you constantly remind me, while groveling, sniveling and begging me to take you back! TAKE YOU BACK!!? WE DATED BRIEFLY!!

OTTO. Finished? *(Otto drinks a second Yoo-hoo.)*

SERGE. NO I AM NOT FINISHED!!! I don't know what to do — tell me what to do. I know you have needs. I know you have problems, you have obvious problems! But this is not fair! I HAVE NEEDS AND PROBLEMS TOO! THIS ISN'T FAIR! DO YOU HEAR ME? THIS JUST IS NOT FAIR!! *(A long pause.)*

OTTO. *(Very small.)* I don't see what you're so worked up about. I just dropped by. I brought some doughnuts. That's all. *(The phone rings.)*

SERGE. ANSWER IT!

OTTO. Excuse me. *(Into the phone:.)* Hello?... Oh, hello.... No, we are NOT back together yet!!... Yes, I understand that I'm a heap of human debris, that I'm not getting any younger and that everything I touch turns to shit!... Well, if that's what you want, I can't stop you from killing yourself.... No, I d*on't* care that you've taken forty-five sleeping pills!!... If you want to die, it's your prerogative.... No, I'm not calling 911 for you!!... I DON'T CARE!... THEN JUST DIE! DIE! DIE AND LEAVE ME ALONE! I CAN'T GO ON LIKE THIS! *(He slams the phone down.)* It was my analyst.

SERGE. What?

OTTO. I'm sorry if I intruded. You keep telling me to get on with my life. For years now, you've been telling me that. "Get on with your life." ... But you are my life.

SERGE. Don't be pathetic.

OTTO. If it's pathetic, it's pathetic. If it's sick or sad or whatever it is — it is the way it is. I love you. And you will love me again. Someday ... or you won't. But I don't intend to give up trying. I see no advantage in surrender.

SERGE. *(After a moment.)* You keep telling me, I'll love you again. But I *never* loved you.

OTTO. What?

SERGE. But I am in love. Now. For the first time. Do you understand me? He's on his way over here right now. He went to get his things and he's coming here, to live. So you simply have to go. *(Sadly Otto rises. The phone rings. Otto looks at Serge, who gestures that Otto should answer it.)*

OTTO. *(Into the phone.)* Hello?... It's for you.

SERGE. *(Taking the phone.)* Hello?... Oh.... I see ... well, but ... but ... *(He hangs up the phone.)* He's not coming.

OTTO. *(Simply.)* Oh. *(Pause, then with great cheer:)* So? Can I stay?

BLACKOUT

41

SCENE 3

FATTY AND SKINNY LAY IN BED

The lights come up on the Dolor living room. It is morning, perhaps we hear the sounds of birds. The doorbell rings. After a moment, the person on the other side begins pounding the door, rather violently. Finally, Amanda enters, wearing a shorty nightgown.

AMANDA.   Coming! *(She goes to the door and opens it, revealing Serge.)* Can I help you?
SERGE.   Is this Ford Dolor's apartment?
AMANDA.   Why do you ask?
SERGE.   It is, isn't it?
AMANDA.   It's nine in the morning.
SERGE.   May I come in?
AMANDA.   No! *(Serge pushes past her. She follows.)*
SERGE.   Where is he?
AMANDA.   Ford's asleep. What is this about?
SERGE.   I'd like to speak to Ford, please.
AMANDA.   Well, I'm not going to wake him. Who are you?!
SERGE.   My name is Serge. Who are you?
AMANDA.   I'm Amanda. I'm Ford's wife. Now, please leave.
SERGE.   Not until I speak to Ford.
AMANDA.   I've asked you to leave. I'd appreciate it if you'd just —
SERGE.   I'm in love with your husband.
AMANDA.   *(Stunned.)* What?
SERGE.   I think. If he's in love with me, that is. If not then I'm not. I'm not putting myself in *that* position.
AMANDA.   You're...?
SERGE.   I'm sorry. I didn't mean to blurt it out like that. I have no intention of hurting you. I have no interest in you. I didn't even make a mental note of your name.

AMANDA. It's Amanda.

SERGE. Would you do me a favor and get Ford? Tell him I'm here.

AMANDA. You're a man.

SERGE. Yes, I know that. I'm aware of that.

AMANDA. You're saying Ford is —

SERGE. My lover. Ford is my lover.

AMANDA. *(Stricken.)* I see.

SERGE. He never mentioned he was married.

AMANDA. He didn't?

SERGE. How long have you been together?

AMANDA. Oh a long time. Several years.

SERGE. Well, he doesn't talk much.

AMANDA. Yes, I know.

SERGE. He's pretty quiet.

AMANDA. He never mentioned you, either.

SERGE. I really didn't come here to upset you. I came to see Ford. I want to find out where we stand. I have plans to make, things to do. I have an appointment at the tanning salon at ten and I intend to know what's going —

AMANDA. How long have you known my husband, Mr. — ?

SERGE. Serge, please.

AMANDA. How long, *Serge?*

SERGE. We met two weeks ago.

AMANDA. I see. And at what sordid, little social club was this?

SERGE. Bloomingdales.

AMANDA. Typical.

SERGE. I'm a model. Maybe you recognize me?

AMANDA. I'm afraid not.

SERGE. Well, I don't do much print work.

AMANDA. That is too bad.

SERGE. I was at Bloomingdales for the fall promotions of the new Calvin Klein underwear. Ford was shopping. He remarked on the cut of my briefs and one thing led to another. We went back to my place, and I found that I could open up to him. I could really talk to him in a way I can't talk to a lot of people. You know most people look at me and they just see someone who's unusually attractive. Then they find out that I'm a model, and they assume that I'm an idiot! You know, I think that's a form of prejudice! Wouldn't you say so?

AMANDA.   I don't know. I don't know *and* I don't care.

SERGE.   Well, we went back to my place. We were talking and listening to some old Donna Summer tapes. And then, we didn't even discuss it — before we knew what was happening we were fucking and sucking and going like rabid dogs in the summer sun, right there in the window!

AMANDA.   Oh my God.

SERGE.   I know. It's pretty undignified, huh?

AMANDA.   Oh my God.

SERGE.   But when you connect, you connect.

AMANDA.   I feel sick.

SERGE.   Oh, we were safe. Not to worry. I consider myself extremely responsible.

AMANDA.   *(Weakly.)* Good.

SERGE.   And that was it. We spent the next fourteen days together.

AMANDA.   Did you?

SERGE.   In bed, on the floor, in the tub, on the roof —

AMANDA.   The roof?

SERGE.   We only stopped for salt tablets! I was seeing someone else, this guy, Roger — and he had heart surgery last week, but I'll be honest with you, Ford made me forget all about Roger. I mean, I forgot to send flowers or call the hospital or anything. I wonder if he lived. Can I use your phone?

AMANDA.   No.

SERGE.   Oh well. It doesn't matter. I never really cared for Roger. He was wild about me but he talked non-stop! I couldn't get a word in edge-wise. With Ford, it was different. We have something very, very unique —

AMANDA.   You can't qualify unique. It either is, or it isn't.

SERGE.   What?

AMANDA.   Skip it.

SERGE.   That's why I don't understand! This might come as a surprise, but Ford was planning on moving in with me. He left my place last night at about twelve and said he'd be back in a couple of hours with his stuff.

AMANDA. He was going to —

SERGE. Then he calls at two in the morning, and no explanation! No excuse! No nothing! Just "I'm not coming." Well I'm not used to this! I'm not used to being treated like a piece of gum stuck under a chair! I want to see him. Now! *(Amanda blocks the hallway.)*

AMANDA. Too bad.

SERGE. I'll wait.

AMANDA. Just go!

SERGE. Tell me, did he say anything? Did he talk about me? Did you discuss it? Was it me? Was I suffocating? Is that it? I thought he liked being suffocated! He liked the paddle! He liked the whip! He liked the cat o'nine tails! He even liked the candle wax!

AMANDA. STOP IT! STOP IT! STOP IT!

SERGE. He told me we had something special! He told me that he loved me!!

AMANDA. *(Bitter.)* When was that?

SERGE. Over and over!

AMANDA. Oh?

SERGE. If not in so many words —

AMANDA. Well, Mr. — Serge, he told me he loved me over and over, last night, *IN* so many words!

SERGE. *(Mock casual.)* Really?

AMANDA. YES! Because Ford and I are MARRIED and we DO love each other! So whatever sick, twisted hold you've had on my husband is broken! He clearly regrets having met you and has decided to stay HERE, with ME, his WIFE!

SERGE. You think so?

AMANDA. Did he return to you last night? No. He was in bed with me last night! And that's exactly where he intends to stay!

SERGE. I'd like him to tell me that.

AMANDA. It's over! Why don't you simply leave? Go. Go and get yourself a tan. If you leave now, there'll be no ugly scenes of recrimination.

SERGE. *(Feigning shock.)* Maybe I — do you have a glass of water?

AMANDA.   No.

SERGE.   Please. I'm not used to this. I'm strikingly attractive and this comes as quite a blow.

AMANDA.   Drink it. Then leave. *(Exasperated, Amanda exits to fetch Serge a drink. He takes the moment to head towards the bedroom. Just as he gets there, Otto appears at the door, which had been left ajar, carrying a bag of groceries and pointing a gun at his temple.)*

OTTO.   THE WORLD IS A RANCID CESSPOOL AND I CAN TAKE IT NO LONGER!!

SERGE.   *(Turning.)* Otto!?

OTTO.   LET MY DEATH BE ON YOUR HEAD, SERGE STUBIN! LET YOUR DREAMS BE FILLED WITH VISIONS OF MY BLOODY SKULL!

SERGE.   What are you doing here!?

OTTO.   *(Entering.)* I followed you. *(Amanda hands Serge a glass of water.)*

SERGE.   Oh dear God.

OTTO.   When you threw me out last night, I slept in the garbage can outside your building. I ate orange rinds and an old shoe for breakfast — alright, alright I went home and had bacon and ~~a dozen~~ eggs — but I was up at seven A.M. and perched outside your house! I followed you! ~~I'd've been here sooner, but that pig at the gun store refused to cash my check! A clear case of anti-Semitism!~~ I haven't been to sleep, but then I never sleep. I haven't slept in years! *(He falls to his knees.)* Do you think you could love me again if I got a good night's sleep? Do you? — Don't answer! I know what you're going to say. You're going to say "No." That's all you ever say: No, no, no, no, no. ~~You are positively monosyllabic!~~ You should buy a word-a-day calendar to build your vocabulary — I tossed and turned all night long and I have decided that life is simply not worth living WHILE YOU LOVE SOMEONE ELSE! — It's unbelievably hot in here! Is anyone else hot? It's like a sauna. ~~I'm waiting for the boy to come around with the cold-water hose for my wrists and temples,~~ for God's sake!

AMANDA.   Do you know this person?

SERGE.   No. No, I don't. We've never met. Call the police.

OTTO.   I am Otto Woodnick!

AMANDA.   You're not!?

SERGE.   He is.

OTTO.   I am!

AMANDA.   Otto! It's me! Betty Pemberton! I was in your home-room class in New Rochelle High!

OTTO.   Betty?!

AMANDA.   Amanda now. Amanda Dolor!

OTTO.   You were so fat!

AMANDA.   You were so thin!

OTTO and AMANDA.   What happened to you!!? *(Otto and Amanda embrace. Serge watches this. As they are embraced, Ford staggers groggily into the room. He sees the scene, has no apparent reaction, turns and exits unnoticed.)*

OTTO.   You look fantastic!

AMANDA.   I've lost some weight. That's all.

OTTO.   I heard about your mother.

AMANDA.   Oh yes.

OTTO.   I'm so sorry.

AMANDA.   Oh don't be, please. My mother was a horrible person really. For years now I've tried to convince myself that her death was somehow tragic to me, that she was a fine person. But she wasn't and it wasn't. She made me feel completely inadequate. She was very beautiful, you know. And tall and thin. She looked like Audrey Hepburn. I hated her. Her death was my liberation.

SERGE.   You hated Audrey Hepburn?!

AMANDA.   God no. I hated my mother. After she died I flourished for the first time. I lost all my weight and took control of my future.

SERGE.   The two of you should start a club! He drones on all the time about his mother.

OTTO.   She's a nightmare!

SERGE.   What's wrong with you people?

AMANDA.   Do you like your mother?

SERGE.   Of course!

OTTO and AMANDA.   Why?

47

SERGE.   She's my mother. I love her. She's charming and witty and she believes in me. She instilled in me the confidence that lets me do anything I put my mind to.

OTTO and AMANDA.   Oh.

SERGE.   My father, on the other hand, is a turd.

OTTO.   Listen to that! He's so pithy. It would take me paragraphs to say what he says with a word! That's the man I love! I hope you don't mind if I have a nibble while we catch up, Betty. I'm starving! I haven't eaten in minutes! *(He pulls a bag of bagels from his bag and eats as he talks.)* Help yourself to a bagel if you want, BUT DON'T TOUCH THE CINNAMON-RAISIN, they're my favorite — I will never forget the first time I saw him! Talk about your some-enchanted-evenings! Do you remember how popular I was in school? I was the best-liked Jewish person in our class. I had more friends than I knew what to do with. Well, I had friends. NO ONE LIKED ME! No one's ever liked me! Do I smell funny? You'd tell me if I smelled funny, wouldn't you , Betty? No, no, don't answer that. I bathe and if I smell funny there's nothing more I can do about it, so I'd just as soon not know it — Where was I? Oh yes, we met at Barneys —

AMANDA.   Department stores are meat markets!

OTTO.   It's so true. Housewares are the worst! Anyway, he took me away with him, for a weekend in Bimini —

SERGE.   I never did any such thing!

OTTO.   Ooooo, he's got a terrible temper!

SERGE.   I've never even been to Bimini!

OTTO.   I think he's capable of anything.

AMANDA.   *I'VE* been to Bimini.

OTTO.   I keep warning him, I keep telling him with that temper and a diet void of sugar, he'll put himself in a grave before he hits twenty!

SERGE.   I'M THIRTY NOW!!

OTTO.   I rest my case.

SERGE.   Get out of my life!

OTTO.   Could you love me again if I got out of your life? Could you?

SERGE.   If you got out of my life? Forever? Yes. Yes, I could.

OTTO.   But then I wouldn't — I'm confused now.

SERGE.   God! *(Amanda takes a bagel from Otto's bag and eats ravenously — it's a cinnamon-raisin.)*

OTTO.   We were going to redecorate his house. We went to Conran's and picked out all new furniture — you look amazing by the way. I can't get over it. You'll have to share your diet tips later — We went to ABC Carpets and found the most precious Persian rugs! We picked china and flatware. I told my mother, who's in traction, by the by, now that you ask. My analyst says I have a neurotic fixation on my mother. But I ask you, at what point does a fixation become neurotic? You be the judge. DO I SEE RAISINS?! *(Amanda drops the bagel, panicked.)* The point is, we made plans. I went so far as to pick up one of those What-Shall-We-Name-the-Baby books. I voted for Shemuel. He wanted Violet. We bickered. I think it was a religious thing. What do you think?

SERGE.   STOP TALKING!!

OTTO.   He tortures me! He's a pig! I weep to dehydration!

AMANDA.   *(Confronting Serge.)* How *can* you be so cruel!? *(Otto crawls to his grocery bag, on the floor and eats.)*

SERGE.   What?

AMANDA.   Look at what you're doing to him!

OTTO.   Yeah, look.

SERGE.   You don't understand the situation.

AMANDA.   How you can function under the elephantine burden of guilt you must carry is a conundrum to me!

SERGE.   A *what?*

OTTO.   I love the way you talk.

AMANDA.   A riddle. It means riddle!

SERGE.   Why don't you just say riddle!?

AMANDA.   Look at the state to which you've reduced this man!

SERGE.   I've reduced him to nothing!

AMANDA.   Exactly my point!

OTTO.   What do you mean by that?

SERGE.   How is this any of your business?

AMANDA.   Loyalty is everything. When I was fat Betty Pemberton, Otto Woodnick came to my aid when no one else cared if I lived or died.

OTTO. I did?

AMANDA. I was teased mercilessly by pretty girls with tiny waists and prematurely perky breasts. I spent many a long afternoon weeping in fat, solitary misery behind the bleachers. There was one group of particularly venomous anorexics. They pelted me with rocks. They stole my English Lit. midterm. Otto Woodnick came to my rescue.

OTTO. I did?

AMANDA. He stayed up all night and helped me redo it! I only got a C+, but I would've had nothing to turn in, if it hadn't been for Otto's gallant chivalry.

OTTO. Don't mention it. Rugelah?

AMANDA. He was sweet and kind and good.

SERGE. Well, he's none of those things now! *(Otto starts choking.)*

AMANDA. And who's fault is that? I know what kind of feral beast you are! You think you can blithely destroy human beings without remuneration. This fat, loud, gasping, wheezing lump of despair — *(Without missing a beat, Amanda kicks Otto, who is choking, on his back. Something flies out of Otto's mouth and back into the bag. He resumes eating, contented. There has been no pause in Amanda's speech.)* — bares no resemblance to the Otto Woodnick I knew! You think I'll let you toy with Ford the way you've toyed with poor, pathetic, now-repulsive Otto?! Well, I'm here to tell you, NO! YOU MAY NOT! You've got to be stopped!

OTTO. Who's Ford?

AMANDA. My husband.

SERGE. My God!

OTTO. *(Rising.)* MY RIVAL!

SERGE. I'm not toying with anyone! I'm in love with Ford —

OTTO. Where is he?

AMANDA. *(Pointing towards the bedroom.)* In there.

SERGE. I think — if he's in love with me —

OTTO. PREPARE TO DIE, YOU FILTHY SCUM! *(Otto stalks off, his gun raised. Serge and Amanda realize what has just hap-*

pened and stand frozen in terror. A moment passes. Offstage.)
WHERE ARE YOU COWARD! IT'S NO USE HIDING!

AMANDA.   He's probably in the shower! *(She immediately re-grets this reflexive response.)*

OTTO.   *(Offstage.)* Well! I'll just wait!! *(Serge and Amanda relax.)*

AMANDA.   I have asked you to leave. I've told you to leave. If I must, I'll call the police.

SERGE.   I'll leave when Ford tells me to.

AMANDA.   What does it take to —

SERGE.   You've said a lot of terrible things to me. Things you have no right to say. You don't know anything about me.

AMANDA.   I know more than I care to, thank you.

SERGE.   You look at me and see someone in control. Someone who's got it all together. You don't know what it's been like.

AMANDA.   *(Sarcastic.)* Enlighten me.

SERGE.   As long as I can remember, since I was a kid, people have constantly thrown themselves at me. Otto's just one extreme case —

AMANDA.   My heart bleeds for you.

SERGE.   It's a curse! Wherever I go, it's just the same! Men, women, children for God's sake! I've spent night after night with hundreds of strangers. Thousands! Millions!

AMANDA.   Is the touching part coming?

SERGE.   Yes — I don't toy with people. I sit and listen to them profess their love for me till I could vomit! — But I never respond. I never say a thing. If absolutely pressed, I tell them, I confess, that I feel nothing. Because that's what I feel. Nothing. I've never felt a thing. I've wanted to. I've tried to. But there's just ... nothing. *(He is working himself into a distraught state.)* And yet, I attract people night and day. I never know what to do with them: the faceless throng of babbling strangers. Until Ford. It's not fair! It's just not fair. Is it my fault that their lives are so obviously empty? Is it my fault that people are simply sucked into me like a vacuum?

AMANDA.   *(Genuinely sympathetic.)* No.

SERGE.   I have needs. I have problems. Does anyone ever

really care about me? No. I seem to attract only the most destructive, broken, needy, sad, sad, sad human beings. What's wrong with me?

AMANDA. *(At a loss for words.)* I'm sure there's nothing wrong with you.

SERGE. Is it my fault I'm unusually attractive?

AMANDA. Of course not.

SERGE. Is it my fault I have beautiful hair?

AMANDA. How could it be?

SERGE. Is it my fault I have nearly perfect skin, straight, white teeth and a smooth, tan stomach as hard as Formica? *(Their eyes meet.)*

AMANDA. I don't, I, well, I wouldn't, I —

SERGE. Am I to blame for my well-muscled thighs?

AMANDA. Nu-uh.

SERGE. Did I ask for my lips? Did I ask for eyes this blue? Am I to be held responsible for my butt — did you happen to notice my butt?

AMANDA. Yes, I did.

SERGE. My life has been a horrible, endless nightmare of empty, hot, pulsating, sweaty, throbbing, wild-dog anonymous sex!

AMANDA. FUCK ME!! *(She lunges at him. They kiss. It is quite passionate. Ford enters in a bathrobe. his hair is wet.)*

FORD. *(Quietly, without emotion.)* Who, um, who's that fat person sobbing in our bathroom? *(Amanda and Serge break their embrace.)*

AMANDA. Ford!

SERGE. What happened to you last night, Ford?!

AMANDA. I know what this looks like.

SERGE. I waited and waited! Did you, or did you not say you'd be right back?

AMANDA. You mustn't jump to conclusions.

SERGE. Then you call and say you're not coming. I'm not used to this! I need to know where we stand.

AMANDA. I realize it looks as if we were embraced — and, in fact, we were. True. But not for the reasons you might think. I knew you'd come out of the shower eventually and I seduced Serge, hoping you'd walk in and find us together, in corpus-dilecti, or whatever it's called. I wanted to prove to you that although this "person" may claim to have feelings of some depth for you, he *obviously* does not.

SERGE. What a crock! Ford, I seduced her! I pretended to be sensitive. You know I'm not sensitive. I pretended to be all upset so she'd fall for me and you'd walk in and discover that whatever hold she's got on you is based on deception!

AMANDA. Oh shut up.

SERGE. You shut up!

AMANDA. You shut up!

SERGE. Make me.

AMANDA. Ford, I don't know if I mentioned this, maybe I did, but did you know that when my mother died, I inherited a great deal of *money?* Her father invented the zip-lock bag, and I did. I inherited an enormous amount of money.

SERGE. Ford, did you realize that as a top runway model I spend six months out of every year in Europe on all expense paid trips to Paris, Milan, Madrid and London for the Spring and Fall collections. Of course everyone gets to bring their spouses. *(Otto enters, unnoticed, holding a huge wad of toilet paper, into which he has been sobbing.)*

AMANDA. Ford, I love you.

SERGE. Ford, me too, I think.

OTTO. *(Shooting the gun into the air.)* I demand to be taken seriously!! *(There is a knock at the door as some plaster falls on Otto's head.)*

AMANDA. Excuse me. *(She tosses the bag of bagels at Otto.)* Here, Otto. Eat. *(He does this, as she goes to the door.)* Who is it?

BEA. *(Offstage.)* Is that Amanda?

AMANDA. *(Opening the door.)* Can I help you?

BEA. YOU HUNG UP ON ME!

AMANDA. Pardon me?

BEA. I'm Bea. From the hot-line. I will not tolerate being hung up on!

OTTO. Mother?

BEA. *(Entering.)* Otto?!

OTTO.   What are you doing here?

BEA.   This one hung up on me! Forty-five minutes we talk and she hangs up! For all I know, she's splattered on the sidewalk this morning — you got a glass of water? I got a taste in my mouth like burned, wet feathers. *(Ford exits to fetch Bea a glass of water.)*

SERGE.   I thought you said your mother was in traction?

OTTO.   I was lying. Or kidding. I don't know which.

BEA.   Typical.

AMANDA.   Thank you for coming, but as you can see, I'm fine.

BEA.   You're Serge, aren't you?

SERGE.   Yes.

BEA.   You look just like your picture, only with clothes. I love that picture. You know I carry it in my purse.

SERGE.   I've been told.

BEA.   Does this mean the two of you are back together?

SERGE.   No, Mrs. Woodnick. It does not! *(Ford enters and hands Bea a glass of water.)*

BEA.   Thank you, darling. *(Amanda takes the glass of water away from Bea.)*

AMANDA.   If you don't mind, Mrs. Woodnick —

OTTO.   Mother, you remember Betty Pemberton?

BEA.   Of course! The big fat girl. Oh who could forget her. Repulsive.

AMANDA.   *I* am Betty Pemberton.

BEA.   I thought you were Amanda?

AMANDA.   I'm both.

BEA.   You look fantastic!

OTTO.   Doesn't she?

AMANDA.   Thank you.

BEA.   I heard about your mother —

AMANDA.   Don't mention it —

BEA.   Maybe you could help Otto? Look at him. Yuk. That's right! That's right, Otto! Eat! Keep eating those bagels! Keep shovin' 'em down your fat ugly throat! That's the boy! Maybe if you're lucky, you'll explode and bits of you'll fall all over Broadway — *(Otto points the gun at Bea.)* Ya look good, Otto.

54

You've lost weight, haven't you? It shows up in your face.

AMANDA.   It was very nice of you to stop by, Mrs. Woodnick. I appreciate your concern, but we're actually —

BEA.   What are you doing here anyway, Otto? Shouldn't you be out looking for work? My son was fired recently.

SERGE.   He mentioned it.

OTTO.   I followed Serge.

BEA.   Why Otto? Why do you have ta make such a pest of yourself? What good can come of that? None. Why'd you follow Serge here?

OTTO.   So I could kill Ford.

BEA.   Who's Ford? *(Ford raises his hand.)* I see. Why?

OTTO.   Because Serge is in love with Ford!

BEA.   *(Angry.)* So what good comes of that?! EAT! GO AHEAD EAT! You make no sense when you talk, so eat.

AMANDA.   I apologize for hanging up —

BEA.   You know, Ford, you have the most beautiful name I ever had in my mouth. And, Amanda, or Betty, or whatever the hell you're calling yourself today, I can see why you were so upset. I'd be upset too, if I thought this one was leaving me for him —

AMANDA.   He's not leaving me for anyone!

SERGE.   *(Grabbing Ford's arm.)* He's coming with me!

AMANDA.   *(Grabbing Ford's other arm.)* I HATE YOU!!

SERGE.   Tell her, Ford. Let's go.

OTTO.   Stay with *her,* Ford. She loves you. He stinks.

BEA.   Mind your own business.

OTTO.   If you fall apart, Serge, I'll pick up the pieces! You could love me again, if I picked up the pieces!

SERGE.   *(Releasing Ford, who falls.)* Never!

OTTO.   You could love me again on the rebound!

AMANDA.   *(To Ford.)* Tell him you never want to see him again!

SERGE.   *(To Ford.)* I have a taxi waiting. We could be in bed in 20 minutes. I'll have you hog-tied, horse-whipped and begging for more —

AMANDA.   *(Out of control.)* IF YOU DO NOT SHUT UP I WILL NOT BE RESPONSIBLE FOR MY ACTIONS!! I'M

LIABLE TO KILL SOMEONE! I CAN DO IT, TOO! THIS IS MY HOME! WHAT ARE YOU PEOPLE DOING HERE AT THIS HOUR!? I SHOULD BE ASLEEP! YOU HAVE COME TO DRIVE ME MAD! PERVERTS AND FAT PEOPLE AND STRANGERS FROM THE TELEPHONE! IT CAN NOT BE APPROPRIATE FOR YOU TO BE HERE! I'M CALLING THAT HOT-LINE AND REPORTING YOU! This has been a very bad couple of weeks! What did I do?! I WAS A GOOD GIRL! SO WHY IS GOD PUNISHING ME NOW? — I may have killed some children yesterday, BUT THAT WAS NOT MY FAULT! IT WAS AN ACCIDENT!

SERGE.   You're unbalanced.

AMANDA.   OF COURSE I'M UNBALANCED!! I HAVEN'T EATEN IN A WEEK! FAGGOT!!

OTTO.   Have a bagel.

BEA.   Ya got a biali?

OTTO.   Let me look —

AMANDA.   I WILL NOT BE REDUCED TO THIS GROVEL-ING, WHINING STATE! I WILL NOT BE MISS HAVISHAM!

SERGE.   *(To Ford.)* We could be fucking right now.

AMANDA.   OTTO!!! SHOOT HIM!!

BEA.   STOP IT! God, stop it already with the shouting. Enough already. You're giving me a headache.

AMANDA.   SHOOT HER! SHOOT ME! SHOOT SOMEONE!

BEA.   You listen to me, darling. I have had extensive crisis intervention training, and I *BELIEVE* I can be of some assis-tance.

AMANDA.   *(Collapsing in despair.)* I give up.

BEA.   Ford, you haven't said much and it seems to me that you are the apex of this unfortunate pentagon. Now ... I ask you. Look at Serge. Think before you answer. Would you say you had feeling for him? Would you say you cared for Serge? Would you say you loved him? *(Ford paces and thinks for a very long time before answering.)*

FORD.   *(Nodding.)* Uh-huh.

AMANDA.   *(Under her breath.)* Shoot the fairy, Otto. Shoot the fairy.

BEA.   Quiet!... Now, Ford. Look at Amanda — Who, I'm as-

56

suming has looked better. Would you say you also had feeling for her? Do you love Amanda? *(Ford paces and thinks for a
very long time before answering.)*
FORD.   *(Nodding.)* Uh-huh.
BEA.   *(Sagely.)* I see … I see…. Alright. If I were to ask you
which one you preferred, what would you say? Let's imagine
that the building is on fire and you can only get one of them
out alive. Which one would you save? Which one do you love
more? *(Ford looks at Amanda and Serge, respectively. He paces,
thinks, tries to decide, then gives up.)*
SERGE.   What is the point of —
BEA.   Listen to me. I spend all my time on the phones at
the crisis center. I listen to hundreds of people. And they all
got a different story. But it's only the details that are different. Basically, they all got the same story: they're alone.
They've got nothing. They never found someone who made
them feel, something. I never found someone. Well, I let
someone slip through my fingers, but that's another story. You
are all so lucky. Why choose? Can't you all just love each
other? Must you condemn yourselves to lives of regret and re-
sentment? *(She seems to step out of the play for a moment to make
a grand point:.)* These are miserable times for the artist in
America, spiritually and economically. It seems to me you
should be banding together, not pulling apart.
AMANDA.   *(Pause, then grudgingly.)* I must admit, Serge, I en-
joyed kissing you. Although I found your tongue hyper-active.
SERGE.   My apartment is tiny really and it's terrifically over-
priced. A few years ago it went co-op and I didn't buy in. Now
I regret it.
BEA.   There are seven days in the week and only three of
you.
SERGE.   *(To Amanda.)* I like the way you smell.
AMANDA.   *(To Serge.)* I can tell you have a big penis.
SERGE.   *(Ford smiles at that.)* Thank you.
BEA.   That alright with you, Ford? *(Ford shrugs "sure.")*
OTTO.   WHAT ABOUT MEEEEEEEE!!!!!!!!
AMANDA.   Aw, poor Otto.
OTTO.   It's all very fine for the three of you to realize you're

shallow to the point of convex, but where does that leave me in your polygamist equation?!

SERGE. Out in the cold.

AMANDA. Sorry.

BEA. Don't binge.

OTTO. Where's the justice?! Fuck justice, where's the symmetry?! I HATE ALL OF YOU VERY MUCH!! — I don't mean that — YES I DO MEAN IT!! I AM SO UNHAPPY! I HATE MY BODY! My skin is so stretched out of whack it's all different textures! Everything shakes! I'm afraid to let people see my feet! I have the ugliest feet in the world! I have no nail on my pinkie toe! I'M A FREAK! I hate the smell of me! My teeth are rotting in my mouth! I have to put anti-perspirant on ALL over my body because there's no telling where some new fold of flesh is going to POP up spontaneously! I wish I could hope for a change, but at this point I consider it a triumph just getting through the day! I WILL NOT GO ON LIKE THIS! I CAN NOT GO ON LIKE THIS!! *(Otto inserts the gun into his mouth. There is a long moment during which the others put their hands over their ears and squint, awaiting the bang, terrified only of the noise. Then Bea steps forward and yanks the gun from Otto.)*

BEA. MUST YA PUT EVERYTHING IN YOUR BIG FAT GREASY MOUTH!?

OTTO. Gimmee the gun!

BEA. *(Pointing it at Otto.)* You're outa control, Otto. I should never a' let you get your own apartment. Look at yourself! Ya look like sumthin' got loose from the Macy's Parade!

OTTO. Give me that —

BEA. LISTEN TO ME! From now on you don't leave my sight!

OTTO. But —

BEA. Not for a minute! Startin' tomorrow: sit ups before breakfast! Push-ups before lunch! Five mile walks twice a day and no more mayonnaise! Low fat foods and Diet Coke!

OTTO. But —

BEA. *(Marching him to the door, at gunpoint.)* MOVE! MOVE IT, YA TUB A' GUTS! I'll have ya looking like a HUMAN BE-

ING in a year or two! We'll wire your jaws shut! We'll get ya to a gym. Ya need aerobics — Step aerobics! Jazzercize! We'll get ya one of them "Sweatin to the Oldies" tapes! And a treadmill, and a stationary bike and a Nordic Track and a Soloflex and a Thighmaster! And no snacks! GREENS! GREENS AND COLONICS TWICE A WEEK! GREENS, COLONICS and for God's sake — VERTICAL STRIPES! Everyone looks one hundred percent better in vertical stripes! *(Otto and Bea are gone. Amanda shuts the door. There is a pause.)*

AMANDA. *(Disturbed.)* He should've killed himself.

SERGE. I would've.

FORD. Hmmm.

AMANDA. What time's your appointment?

SERGE. Ten.

AMANDA. *(Rushes to the bedroom.)* That gives us twenty minutes.... Come on! *(She goes into the bedroom, followed by Serge. Ford sits and eats Otto's groceries. We hear Serge and Amanda's lovemaking at once. Offstage.)* Oh God.

SERGE. *(Offstage.)* Oh Christ.

AMANDA. *(Offstage.)* Oh God.

SERGE. *(Offstage.)* Oh Christ.

AMANDA. *(Offstage.)* Oh God!

SERGE. *(Offstage.)* Oh Christ!! *(There is a pause. Offstage.)* Ford!!

AMANDA. We're waiting! *(There is a violent knocking at the front door.)*

OTTO. *(Offstage.)* SERGE! IF I SIT, *QUIET IN THE CORNER* ... COULD YA LOVE ME!!? *(Blackout.)*

END OF PLAY

ALTERNATE ENDING

This is the ending of the play as it was performed at The Woolly Mammoth Theater in Washington DC. The text was ostensibly the same to the point where Ford shrugs in acquiescence to Bea's suggestion that he live with both Amanda and Serge. Otto's reaction, you will see, was quite different.

OTTO.   WHAT ABOUT MEEEEEEEE!!!!!!!!

AMANDA.   Aw, poor Otto.

OTTO.   It's all very fine for the three of you to realize that you're shallow to the point of convex, but where does that leave me in your polygamist equation?!

SERGE.   Out in the cold.

AMANDA.   Sorry.

BEA.   Don't binge.

OTTO.   Oh, I don't care! I just don't care anymore! I've had it. I AM SO UNHAPPY!! I've always been unhappy! You say they're lucky to feel something? Well, I'm not so sure. I feel plenty. I feel everything. And it feels pretty goddamn terrible!

BEA.   Here he goes!

OTTO.   Where's the justice! Fuck justice! Where's the symmetry?!... No one ever liked me. Mother, you carry pictures in your wallet of people you never met, instead of pictures of me!... When I was a child, I was in the sixth grade, I think, we had a dance at my school on the first day of May, a Sadie Hawkins dance. It was silly, it was nothing — is it hot in here as Buchanwald, or what? — Anyway, the girls were supposed to ask the boys to dance. And I was not an unattractive child! Tell them, Mother. I wasn't fat then. I didn't have clubbedfeet or dandruff or anything. I was quite normal-looking, and maybe even a little better than normal-looking. But NO ONE asked me to dance ... no one. The entire dance went by and

60

not one little girl ever came over and asked me to dance. I went to the cloak room and cried and cried. The teacher, Miss MacFarland, I'll never forget her, Miss MacFarland heard me. She came to the cloak room, drawn there by my hideous, shrieking sobs. And she knelt down, next to me, down to where I'd curled myself into the fetal position, on the floor, buried under a mountain of coats. She uncovered me and said.... "Otto? Otto, why are you crying?" I could barely talk. But I spoke in that spastic, convulsive way children do when they're sobbing. I said, "No one will dance with me." She nodded very sagely, the chain that held her glasses around her neck bobbed up and down. And then she said, "Oh." I wasn't satisfied. That wasn't the comfort I needed. I asked her, "Why?" She thought for a very long time. And then she answered me.... "No one likes you, Otto. No one likes you and no one ever will...." Well. It's hard to argue with a figure of such authority as Miss MacFarland. But I knew she was wrong. Or lying. Sometime, somewhere, someday, someone would! I thought Serge did. For a moment — I mean people have pretended to like me, when it suited their needs, if there was something they wanted — help with their homework. But, I thought, Serge ... I thought ... well, it doesn't really matter what I thought at this point, does it?

SERGE.   Not really.

OTTO.   I HATE MY BODY!!! My skin is so stretched out of whack it's all different textures! Everything shakes!! I'm afraid to let people see my feet! I have the ugliest feet in the world! I have no nail on my pinkie toe! I'M A FREAK!! I hate the smell of me! My teeth are rotting in my mouth! I have to put anti-perspirant on ALL over my body because there's no telling where some new fold of flesh is going to POP up, spontaneously! I wish I could hope for a change, but at this point I consider it a triumph just getting through the day! I HATE ALL OF YOU VERY MUCH!! I don't mean that! Now none of you are ever going to like me — YES I DO MEAN IT! None of you are ever going to like me anyway! I gave up on you, Mother, a long time ago! And at this point, Serge, I realize, yes, that YOU are NEVER GOING TO LOVE ME AGAIN!

61

WELL FUCK YOU! That's all I can say! Because I'm never going to love you again either! And THANK GOD! I AM SICK OF YOU! I AM TIRED OF WEARING THIS UNREQUITED LOVE, LIKE A YOKE AROUND MY NECK! I HOPE YOU DIE!... *(With great dignity.)* Now, if you'll excuse me, I'm going to the bathroom, because I FEEL SICK! *(Amanda points, indicating the powder room. Otto exits, grandly and shuts the door behind him.)*

AMANDA. He's unbelievable loquacious.

BEA. You have no idea.

SERGE. I hope he leaves soon. *(There is a gunshot from behind the powder-room door. Amanda, Serge, and Bea rush to the door and open it. Amanda screams in terror and the three of them stand, frozen, horrified, in the powder-room doorway. Ford eats laconically from Otto's grocery bag as the lights fade, slowly, to darkness.)*

END OF PLAY

PROPERTY LIST

SCENE 1

ONSTAGE
DOLOR APARTMENT
Cigarettes (AMANDA)
Lighters (AMANDA)
Cellular phone with speakers (AMANDA)
Yellow pagess (AMANDA)
Stereos (AMANDA)
BEA'S CUBICLE
A bottle of water
Office telephone with headset (BEA)
Clipboard (BEA)
Pencils (BEA)
Magazines
Can of Diet Coke
Needlepoint canvas wit wool and needle

OFF STAGE
Keys (FORD)

SCENE 2

ONSTAGE
Compact disk remote control
Telephone
12 identical jeans (in closet)
12 identical T-shirts (in closet)
12 identical pairs of socks (in closet)

OFFSTAGE

1 bag of groceries containing the following (OTTO):
    bag of pretzel rods
    box of Dunkin' Donuts
    package of Yodels
    box of Oreos
    bag of Cheeze Doodles
    bag of Fritos
    2 bottles of Yoo-hoo
    assorted candy and chips
    1 can of Slim-Fast
    1 box of Sno-Caps

SCENE 3

OFFSTAGE

2 glasses of water (AMANDA, FORD)
1 bag of groceries containing the following (OTTO):
    bag of bagels, both plain and raisin
    bag of rugelah
    assorted snacks
Gun (OTTO)
Wad of toilet paper (OTTO)

COSTUME PLOT

AMANDA
Cream, off-white cropped T-shirt
Beige elastic-waist pants

BEA
Navy-tweed Chanel suit (jacket and skirt)
Navy silk blouse
White silk flower at throat
4 heavy gold necklaces
Wedding ring
Engagement ring
Chanel pumps
Natural stockings
2 gold bracelets
Gold earrings

FORD
Black T-shirt
Black leather jacket
Black jeans
Black boots
Black sunglasses on black cord

SCENE 2

SERGE
Calvin Klein bike-short-style underpants
Silver, hard bracelet

OTTO
Fat suit
Gray suit (size 56 portly; jacket, pants)
White pocket square
Black shoes
Black socks
White shirt
Striped tie with tie clip
Black belt

SCENE 3

AMANDA
Hot pink, baby-doll shorty nightgown
Hot pink ponytail holder

SERGE
Same as Scene 2, add:
    Muscle-style T-shirt, white
    Blue denim jeans
    Tan work boots
    White sweat socks

OTTO
Same as Scene 2

FORD
Black towel
Black silk bathrobe

BEA
Turquoise Chanel suit (jacket and skirt)
Chanel handbag
Accessories remain the same

SOUND EFFECTS

Telephone ring as heard over the phone
Telephone ring as heard in person
Birds
Doorbell
Gunshot

NEW PLAYS

★ **HONOUR by Joanna Murray-Smith.** In a series of intense confrontations, a wife husband, lover and daughter negotiate the forces of passion, history, responsibility and honou "HONOUR makes for surprisingly interesting viewing. Tight, crackling dialogue (usual played out in punchy verbal duels) captures characters unable to deal with emotions ... Murra Smith effectively places her characters in situations that strip away pretense." –*Variety* "... th play's virtues are strong: a distinctive theatrical voice, passionate concerns ... HONOUR mig just capture a few honors of its own." –*Time Out Magazine* [1M, 3W] ISBN: 0-8222-1683-

★ **MR. PETERS' CONNECTIONS by Arthur Miller.** Mr. Miller describes the protagon as existing in a dream-like state when the mind is "freed to roam from real memories to co jectures, from trivialities to tragic insights, from terror of death to glorying in one's bei alive." With this memory play, the Tony Award and Pulitzer Prize-winner reaffirms his statu as the world's foremost dramatist. "... a cross between Joycean stream-of-consciousness a Strindberg's dream plays, sweetened with a dose of William Saroyan's philosophical whin ... CONNECTIONS is most intriguing ..." –*The NY Times* [5M, 3W] ISBN: 0-8222-1687

★ **THE WAITING ROOM by Lisa Loomer.** Three women from different centuries m in a doctor's waiting room in this dark comedy about the timeless quest for beauty – and cost. "... THE WAITING ROOM ... is a bold, risky melange of conflicting elements tha ... terrifically moving ... There's no resisting the fierce emotional pull of the play." –*The Times* "... one of the high points of this year's Off-Broadway season ... THE WAITIℕ ROOM is well worth a visit." –*Back Stage* [7M, 4W, flexible casting] ISBN: 0-8222-1594-2

★ **THE OLD SETTLER by John Henry Redwood.** A sweet-natured comedy about two church-going sisters in 1943 Harlem and the handsome young man who rents a room in their apartment. "For all of its decent sentiments, THE OLD SETTLER avoids sentimentality. It has the authenticity and lack of pretense of an Early American sampler." –*The NY Times* "We've had some fine plays Off-Broadway this season, and this is one of the best." –*The NY Post* [1M, 3W] ISBN: 0-8-222-1642-6

★ **LAST TRAIN TO NIBROC by Arlene Hutton.** In 1940 two young strangers share a seat on a train bound east only to find their paths will cross again. "All aboard. LAST TRAIN TO NIBROC is a sweetly told little chamber romance." –*Show Business* "... [a] gently charming lit-tle play, reminiscent of Thornton Wilder in its look at rustic Americans who are to be treas-ured for their simplicity and directness ..." –*Associated Press* "The old formula of boy with girls, boy loses girl, boy wins girl still works ... [a] well-made play that perfectly captures a slice of small-town-life-gone-by." –*Back Stage* [1M, 1W] ISBN: 0-8222-1753-8

★ **OVER THE RIVER AND THROUGH THE WOODS by Joe DiPietro.** Nick sees both sets of his grandparents every Sunday for dinner. This is routine until he has to tell them that he's been offered a dream job in Seattle. The news doesn't sit so well. "A hilarious family comedy that is even funnier than his long running musical revue *I Love You, You're Perfect, Now Change.*" –*Back Stage* "Loaded with laughs every step of the way." –*Star-Ledger* [3M, 3W] ISBN: 0-8222-1712-0

★ **SIDE MAN by Warren Leight.** 1999 Tony Award winner. This is the story of a broken family and the decline of jazz as popular entertainment. "... a tender, deeply personal memo-ry play about the turmoil in the family of a jazz musician as his career crumbles at the dawn of the age of rock-and-roll ..." –*The NY Times* "[SIDE MAN] is an elegy for two things – a lost world and a lost love. When the two notes sound together in harmony, it is moving and grace-ful ..." –*The NY Daily News* "An atmospheric memory play ... with crisp dialogue and clear-ly drawn characters ... reflects the passing of an era with persuasive insight ... The joy and despair of the musicians is skillfully illustrated." –*Variety* [5M, 3W] ISBN: 0-8222-1721-X

DRAMATISTS PLAY SERVICE, INC.
440 Park Avenue South, New York, NY 10016 212-683-8960 Fax 212-213-1539
postmaster@dramatists.com www.dramatists.com

NEW PLAYS

★ **CLOSER by Patrick Marber.** Winner of the 1998 Olivier Award for Best Play and the 1999 New York Drama Critics Circle Award for Best Foreign Play. Four lives intertwine over the course of four and a half years in this densely plotted, stinging look at modern love and betrayal. "CLOSER is a sad, savvy, often funny play that casts a steely, unblinking gaze at the world of relationships and lets you come to your own conclusions ... CLOSER does not merely hold your attention; it burrows into you." –*New York Magazine* "A powerful, darkly funny play about the cosmic collision between the sun of love and the comet of desire." –*Newsweek Magazine* [2M, 2W] ISBN: 0-8222-1722-8

★ **THE MOST FABULOUS STORY EVER TOLD by Paul Rudnick.** A stage manager, headset and prompt book at hand, brings the house lights to half, then dark, and cues the creation of the world. Throughout the play, she's in control of everything. In other words, she's either God, or she thinks she is. "Line by line, Mr. Rudnick may be the funniest writer for the stage in the United States today ... One-liners, epigrams, withering put-downs and flashing repartee: These are the candles that Mr. Rudnick lights instead of cursing the darkness ... a testament to the virtues of laughing ... and in laughter, there is something like the memory of Eden." –*The NY Times* "Funny it is ... consistently, rapaciously, deliriously ... easily the funniest play in town." –*Variety* [4M, 5W] ISBN: 0-8222-1720-1

★ **A DOLL'S HOUSE by Henrik Ibsen, adapted by Frank McGuinness.** Winner of the 1997 Tony Award for Best Revival. "New, raw, gut-twisting and gripping. Easily the hottest drama this season." –*USA Today* "Bold, brilliant and alive." –*The Wall Street Journal* "A thunderclap of an evening that takes your breath away." –*Time Magazine* [4M, 4W, 2 boys] ISBN: 0-8222-1636-1

★ **THE HERBAL BED by Peter Whelan.** The play is based on actual events which occurred in Stratford-upon-Avon in the summer of 1613, when William Shakespeare's elder daughter was publicly accused of having a sexual liaison with a married neighbor and family friend. "In his probing new play, THE HERBAL BED ... Peter Whelan muses about a sidelong event in the life of Shakespeare's family and creates a finely textured tapestry of love and lies in the early 17th-century Stratford." –*The NY Times* "It is a first rate drama with interesting moral issues of truth and expediency." –*The NY Post* [5M, 3W] ISBN: 0-8222-1675-2

★ **SNAKEBIT by David Marshall Grant.** A study of modern friendship when put to the test. "... a rather smart and absorbing evening of water-cooler theater, the intimate sort of Off-Broadway experience that has you picking apart the recognizable characters long after the curtain calls." – *The NY Times* "Off-Broadway keeps on presenting us with compelling reasons for going to the theater. The latest is SNAKEBIT, David Marshall Grant's smart new comic drama about being thirtysomething and losing one's way in life." –*The NY Daily News* [3M, 1W] ISBN: 0-8222-1724-4

★ **A QUESTION OF MERCY by David Rabe.** The Obie Award-winning playwright probes the sensitive and controversial issue of doctor-assisted suicide in the age of AIDS in this poignant drama. "There are many devastating ironies in Mr. Rabe's beautifully considered, piercingly clear-eyed work ..." –*The NY Times* "With unsettling candor and disturbing insight, the play arouses pity and understanding of a troubling subject ... Rabe's provocative tale is an affirmation of dignity that rings clear and true." –*Variety* [6M, 1W] ISBN: 0-8222-1643-4

★ **DiMLY PERCEIVED THREATS TO THE SYSTEM by Jon Klein.** Reality and fantasy overlap with hilarious results as this unforgettable family attempts to survive the nineties. "Here's a play whose point about fractured families goes to the heart, mind – and ears." –*The Washington Post* "... an end-of-the millennium comedy about a family on the verge of a nervous breakdown ... Trenchant and hilarious ..." –*The Baltimore Sun* [2M, 4W] ISBN: 0-8222-1677-9

DRAMATISTS PLAY SERVICE, INC.
440 Park Avenue South, New York, NY 10016 212-683-8960 Fax 212-213-1539
postmaster@dramatists.com www.dramatists.com

NEW PLAYS

★ **AS BEES IN HONEY DROWN by Douglas Carter Beane.** Winner of the John Gassner Playwriting Award. A hot young novelist finds the subject of his new screenplay in a New York socialite who leads him into the world of *Auntie Mame* and *Breakfast at Tiffany's*, before she takes him for a ride. "A delicious soufflé of a satire … [an] extremely entertaining fable for an age that always chooses image over substance." *–The NY Times* "… A witty assessment of one of the most active and relentless industries in a consumer society … the creation of 'hot' young things, which the media have learned to mass produce with efficiency and zeal." *–The NY Daily News* [3M, 3W, flexible casting] ISBN: 0-8222-1651-5

★ **STUPID KIDS by John C. Russell.** In rapid, highly stylized scenes, the story follows four high-school students as they make their way from first through eighth period and beyond, struggling with the fears, frustrations, and longings peculiar to youth. "In STUPID KIDS … playwright John C. Russell gets the opera of adolescence to a T … The stylized teenspeak of STUPID KIDS … suggests that Mr. Russell may have hidden a tape recorder under a desk in study hall somewhere and then scoured the tapes for good quotations … it is the kids' insular, ceaselessly churning world, a pre-adult world of Doritos and libidos, that the playwright seeks to lay bare." *–The NY Times* "STUPID KIDS [is] a sharp-edged … whoosh of teen angst and conformity anguish. It is also very funny." *–NY Newsday* [2M, 2W] ISBN: 0-8222-1698-1

★ **COLLECTED STORIES by Donald Margulies.** From Obie Award-winner Donald Margulies comes a provocative analysis of a student-teacher relationship that turns sour when the protégé becomes a rival. "With his fine ear for detail, Margulies creates an authentic, insular world, and he gives equal weight to the opposing viewpoints of two formidable characters." *–The LA Times* "This is probably Margulies' best play to date …" *–The NY Post* "… always fluid and lively, the play is thick with ideas, like a stock-pot of good stew." *–The Village Voice* [2W] ISBN: 0-8222-1640-X

★ **FREEDOMLAND by Amy Freed.** An overdue showdown between a son and his father sets off fireworks that illuminate the neurosis, rage and anxiety of one family – and of America at the turn of the millennium. "FREEDOMLAND's more obvious links are to *Buried Child* and *Bosoms and Neglect*. Freed, like Guare, is an inspired wordsmith with a gift for surreal touches in situations grounded in familiar and real territory." *–Curtain Up* [3M, 4W] ISBN: 0-8222-1719-8

★ **STOP KISS by Diana Son.** A poignant and funny play about the ways, both sudden and slow, that lives can change irrevocably. "There's so much that is vital and exciting about STOP KISS … you want to embrace this young author and cheer her onto other works … the writing on display here is funny and credible … you also will be charmed by its heartfelt characters and up-to-the-minute humor." *–The NY Daily News* "… irresistibly exciting … a sweet, sad, and enchantingly sincere play." *–The NY Times* [3M, 3W] ISBN: 0-8222-1731-7

★ **THREE DAYS OF RAIN by Richard Greenberg.** The sins of fathers and mothers make for a bittersweet elegy in this poignant and revealing drama. "… a work so perfectly judged it heralds the arrival of a major playwright … Greenberg is extraordinary." *–The NY Daily News* "Greenberg's play is filled with graceful passages that are by turns melancholy, harrowing, and often, quite funny." *–Variety* [2M, 1W] ISBN: 0-8222-1676-0

★ **THE WEIR by Conor McPherson.** In a bar in rural Ireland, the local men swap spooky stories in an attempt to impress a young woman from Dublin who recently moved into a nearby "haunted" house. However, the tables are soon turned when she spins a yarn of her own. "You shed all sense of time at this beautiful and devious new play." *–The NY Times* "Sheer theatrical magic. I have rarely been so convinced that I have just seen a modern classic. Tremendous." *–The London Daily Telegraph* [4M, 1W] ISBN: 0-8222-1706-6

DRAMATISTS PLAY SERVICE, INC.
440 Park Avenue South, New York, NY 10016 212-683-8960 Fax 212-213-1539
postmaster@dramatists.com www.dramatists.com